WITHDRAWN

THE SINO-SOVIET TERRITORIAL DISPUTE, 1949-64

THE SINO-SOVIET TERRITORIAL DISPUTE, 1949-64

George Ginsburgs

Carl F. Pinkele

PRAEGER PUBLISHERS
Praeger Special Studies

New York • London • Sydney • Toronto

Library of Congress Cataloging in Publication Data

Ginsburgs, George.
　　The Sino-Soviet territorial dispute, 1949-64.

　　Bibliography: p.
　　1. China--Boundaries--Russia. 2. Russia--Boundaries--China. I. Pinkele, Carl F., joint author. II. Title.
DS740.5.R8G48　　　911'.51　　　78-19458
ISBN 0-03-027096-0

DS
740.5
R8
G48
1978

PRAEGER PUBLISHERS
PRAEGER SPECIAL STUDIES
383 Madison Avenue, New York, N.Y. 10017, U.S.A.

Published in the United States of America in 1978
by Praeger Publishers,
A Division of Holt, Rinehart and Winston, CBS, Inc.

89　038　987654321

© 1978 by Praeger Publishers

All rights reserved

Printed in the United States of America

PREFACE

The aim of the present study is to examine the official record of the Sino-Soviet polemics concerning the geography of their shared boundary line and related territorial claims from the stylistic point of view in order to: 1) determine the kind of technical formulas the two countries have invoked in the course of the argument to establish their respective positions on the subject; 2) identify other relevant items that might have been used in this connection and perhaps were not; 3) where appropriate, suggest reasons for this selective method and trace their roots to pertinent doctrinal, historical, political, strategic/tactical, and similar considerations; and 4) assess the evidence derived from the tone and tenor of the debate in terms of the light it sheds on the substantive nature of the dispute, that is, does the pattern of verbal communication support the contention that the controversy stems from real, concrete issues and therefore reflects a tense, conflict-pregnant situation, or does the rhetoric fit the opposite thesis which maintains that the entire episode involves more sound effects than solid content.

The critical focus, then, is not on the intrinsic validity and merits of the legal concepts and principles that each side has relied upon to build its case on this occasion, and the inquiry does not propose to reach conclusions about which party has a "superior" stake measured by the "objective standards of international law." Instead, the intent is to analyze the dynamics of resort to international law artifacts by a pair of self-appointed "socialist" states in the context of a common quarrel, ostensibly over frontiers and title to land, so as to answer the following questions: what use did the corresponding governments make of the recognized norms of international law in such a contingency; what role did they assign to international law as a body of rules applicable to the settlement of differences between sovereign members of the global community; what importance did they seem to attach to the business of justifying their attitude or behavior with reference to the accepted canon of international law precedent and practice; how are these actions and perceptions likely to affect efforts at the eventual disposition of the problem; is the matter being handled in the same way that two "nonsocialist" states or a "socialist" and a "nonsocialist" state would perform under these circumstances or, if not, how and why; assuming they exist, what bearing will these unique elements have on the subsequent conduct of the contestants, their respective definitions of a desirable modus vivendi, and their ultimate approach to the operational aspects of devising a solution that would accommodate the basic requirements and meet the essential needs of all concerned. In short, this is an investigation into the procedural features of the incident and the corollary themes: 1) how, in this instance, form has influenced substance and vice versa; for example, did the choice of vocabulary add fuel to the fire or help contain the flames, did the oral and written signals accompanying the physical phenomena strive to cool tempers or rub salt into the wounds inflicted by the latter; 2) hence, whether the thrust of the diplomatic dialogue which paralleled these developments puts a different color on the picture from the one that the bare facts tend to convey; and, 3) should a marked divergence emerge between word and deed, which of these indicia is to be attributed greater weight or probative value, and how does an observer of the scene seek to reconcile the competing versions.

The results will not show that Moscow or Peking is the more virtuous party in a juridical sense. However, the account will illuminate how and when the Soviet and Chinese leaderships have in this affair espoused the institutions of international law, which of its propositions they have felt free to advocate, and also what substitute prescriptions they have tried to insinuate into the record when a suitable opportunity offered itself to further their own advantage by this artifice. Most important, this data should, in turn, make it possible to tell with better documentation and higher certainty if the fracas over the profile of their joint frontier and the status of the border territories is prompted by serious causes and has a genuine raison d'être or, on the contrary, rates mainly as a sham contraption pressed into service for quite extraneous ends.

ACKNOWLEDGMENTS

The authors wish to express their gratitude to the Harvard University Press and the American Society of International Law for permission to make use of their study "The Genesis of the Territorial Issue in the Sino-Soviet Dialogue: Substantive Dispute or Ideological Pas de Deux?" in J. A. Cohen (ed.), China's Practice of International Law, Harvard University Press, Cambridge, Mass., 1972, pp. 167-238.

CONTENTS

	Page
PREFACE	v
ACKNOWLEDGMENTS	vi

Chapter

1   BACKGROUND   1

     Article 55 of the Common Program, 1949   1
     The Treaty of Friendship, Alliance, and Mutual
        Aid, 1950   5
     The Sino-Soviet Discussions of 1954   6
     The Sino-Soviet Discussions of 1957   9
     Border Corrections Probe—Buz-Aigyr, 1960   12
     Conclusions   17
     Summary   24
     Notes   25

2   THE SOVIET OFFENSIVE   35

     Khrushchev's Speech to the Supreme Soviet, 1962   35
     The Soviet Reaction to the Chinese-Indian Dispute   39
     Khrushchev's Tactics: Two Hypotheses   40
     Chinese Reaction   44
     The Soviet Response: Counterattack or Negotiate?   48
     Notes   59

3   STALEMATE   67

     PRC Shatters Public Silence over Sinkiang, 1963   68
     The Soviet Side to the Sinkiang Issue   70
     The Soviet Policy Paper, 1963   72
     The Border River Issue: A Retrospective Note   75
     The Soviet Propaganda Battle   79
        CPSU Letter, November 29, 1963   80
        Khrushchev's Letter, December 21, 1963   82
     PRC Reaction to Soviet Bid   86

Chapter		Page
	An Analysis of the Soviet Communication	88
	Notes	90
4	THE 1964 CONFERENCE	95
	Preliminary Skirmishes	95
	The 1964 Affair: The Chinese Side	98
	The 1964 Affair: The Soviet Side	100
	The 1964 Conference: Further Analysis	101
	The Norms of International Law	103
	Current Status of Contested Areas	105
	The Thalweg	106
	The Soviet Impetus	111
	The PRC's Response	113
	The Chinese Take the Initiative	117
	PRC Claims Are Raised at an Official Public Level	118
	Territorial Dispute vs. Territorial Conflict	124
	Conclusion	128
	Notes	132
SELECTIVE BIBLIOGRAPHY		139
ABOUT THE AUTHORS		146

THE SINO-SOVIET TERRITORIAL DISPUTE, 1949-64

1

BACKGROUND

As we have gradually learned, the topic of frontier "adjustments" is not an entirely new item on the record of the Soviet and Chinese Communist governments' diplomatic business with one another.

ARTICLE 55 OF THE COMMON PROGRAM, 1949

In principle, the advent of the Chinese Communist party to power on the mainland should not have caused any undue difficulties along the Sino-Soviet border. True, Article 55 of the Common Program of the Chinese People's Political Consultative Conference of September 29, 1949,[1] had declared that "the Central People's Government of the People's Republic of China shall study the treaties and agreements concluded between the Kuomintang and foreign governments, and shall recognize, abrogate, revise, or renegotiate them according to their respective contents." The dictum presumably applied to all the states concerned, not exempting the Soviet Union, and to all manner of agreements, frontier pacts included. Yet, the precise effect of that clause on the position of the Soviet Union's existing borders with the People's Republic of China (PRC) remains unclear.

In the first place, it should be pointed out, this key formula expressly encompassed only "the treaties and agreements concluded between the Kuomintang and foreign governments." As against that, the Soviet Union's operative boundary line with the PRC does not owe its origins to any accords entered into with the Kuomintang administration, leaving the Mongolian question aside for a minute.[2] Indeed, even in their Agreement on General Principles for the Settlement of Problems of May 31, 1924,[3] (which, though signed with a predecessor of the Kuomintang regime, nevertheless continued to regulate relations between the Soviet Union and China following the Kuomintang's accession to power), the contracting states merely confirmed that they would "redemarcate their national boundaries" at a conference scheduled to be held within one month from that day to "conclude and carry out the detailed arrangements." These arrangements, in turn, would be completed as soon as possible and, in any case, not later than six months from the date of the opening of the parley. "Pending such redemarcation," the parties agreed "to maintain the present boundaries."[4] However, the conference, which should have met almost at once, was not staged until 1925 and, it is now recalled, "owing to the historical conditions at the time, no agreement was reached by the two sides on the boundary question, no redemarcation of the boundary between the two countries was made, and no new equal treaty was concluded by the two countries."[5]

Thus, while the 1924 agreement spoke elsewhere of the decision of the parties to annul at the proposed session "all conventions, treaties, agreements, protocols, contracts, etc., on the basis of equality, reciprocity, and justice, as well as the spirit of the Declarations of the Soviet Government of the years 1919 and 1920," nothing came of these grandiose plans, and the old location of the frontier stayed unchanged. Manchukuo rose and fell, pitched battles were fought between Soviet and Japanese forces over where the boundary should run in certain sections, but to no avail: the territorial status quo was not seriously disturbed throughout.

The Mongolian affair constitutes an exception. By accepting in the exchange of notes with the Soviet Union of August 14, 1945,[6] to recognize the independence of Outer Mongolia "in her existing boundaries," if a plebiscite conducted after the defeat of Japan showed it to be the wish of the local population, and by honoring its promise when that condition was subsequently fulfilled, the Kuomintang regime, in concert with the Soviet authorities, sanctioned the removal of the issue of defining the central portion of the erstwhile Sino-Soviet frontier from their common agenda. Henceforth, the Soviet Union and the Mongolian People's Republic (MPR) would be responsible for determining the configuration of the MPR's northern contour, and China and the MPR would fix the limits of the latter's southern confines.

This transaction clearly lay within the scope of the concept ultimately solidified in the language of the aforecited Article 55, to the premises of which the Chinese Communist leadership must have subscribed from the outset. This feature may explain why, virtually from the first moment of the PRC's inception and almost simultaneously with the inauguration of USSR-PRC ties, the topic of Mongolia intruded into the picture. For Soviet sources have recently revealed that, already in 1949, "Mao Tse-tung in a purely chauvinistic spirit confronted the Soviet leadership with the 'problem' of merging the MPR with China."[7] Assuming the report is true, this bid (like those that followed) met with a flat Soviet rejection and failed. Rather, the

BACKGROUND

contrary Soviet view seems to have prevailed and, in light of these curious developments, it may well be that Soviet insistence on making the record clear on that score is in fact responsible for the eventual adoption of an extra safeguard to that effect. At any rate, the Soviet Union and the PRC, in an exchange of notes of February 14, 1950,[8] did think it advisable to reconfirm officially the existing arrangement by arriving at a fresh understanding in which both countries formally acknowledged that "the independent status of the Mongolian People's Republic is fully guaranteed as a result of the referendum held in Outer Mongolia in 1945, which attested to its desire for independence and as a result of the Chinese People's Republic's establishment of diplomatic relations with it."

In roundabout fashion, the Soviets thus got the Communist Chinese to sanction, if not the letter, at least the juridical consequences of the 1945 correspondence pertaining to Mongolia. While the Treaty of Friendship and Alliance and the Agreement on the Chinese Eastern Railroad, Dairen, and Port Arthur of August 14, 1945, and all the documents appended thereto, were then explicitly voided, the companion communications concerning Mongolia were never mentioned and, instead, Peking's constructive acquiescence in the outcome of the 1945 plebiscite amounted practically to acceptance on its part "to inherit" the underlying agreement. Significantly, the latest messages did not repeat the earlier reference to (and ensuing endorsement of) Mongolia's "existing borders." The core problem of Mongolia's right to its own legal personality, though, seemed finally to have been put to rest.

Nevertheless, the important thing about this episode resides precisely in the element that an express guarantee was somehow deemed necessary in 1950 to allay possible doubts regarding the MPR's future lot. Either the PRC's purported assertion of proprietary title to Mongolia in 1949, or perhaps its espousal on that occasion of theories which were later spelled out in the notorious Article 55, rendered any reliance on the notion of automatic succession by the PRC to the 1945 blueprint a high-risk proposition. Hence, caution presumably prompted a determined effort by the Soviet Union to cure the major defect in the MPR's present legal status vis-a-vis Peking by extracting from the latter a special pledge to abide by the status quo here and, in a positive sense, consent to be bound by the terms of an accord entered into by its predecessor.[9] Certainly, the incident suggests that a formula akin to Article 55 operated in this instance and illuminates how the problem raised by that device was handled in this specific case. The operation inferentially also lends credence to the story that the PRC had at once proceeded to stake a claim to Mongolia (or, at least, had demonstrated a sufficiently ambiguous attitude toward the preceding modus vivendi) through circumstantial evidence showing that at the time measures were indeed implemented of the sort that would act to cancel any such move, either in anticipation of this kind of an attempt or because the attempt had in fact already been made and had to be countered forthwith as a concrete item of current business.

In the second place, the language of Article 55 is permissive, not mandatory. The successor regime thereby simply served notice on all states which had in the past signed treaties and agreements with the Kuomintang administration that it considered itself free to scrutinize the substance of these instruments and to reach appropriate conclusions whether to keep them in force, amend them, or supplant them with a different text. No a priori or automatic negation of the international obligations incurred by the preceding sovereign was presently envisaged, but rather an ad hoc process of critical review of the pertinent materials would objectively disclose which of these agreements could be retained by the PRC, which had to undergo minor surgery to fit its revolutionary philosophy, and which were beyond salvation. Since no time limit was set for accomplishing the job of "sorting out" the collection of treaties surviving from the Kuomintang era, the fate of these documents meanwhile remained in doubt.

Still, the impression one gathers is that, technically, all such agreements remained valid until properly denounced or suitably modified by the PRC leadership. The observation holds doubly true for the category of border pacts. Indeed, no less a figure than Chou En-lai reportedly indicated as much in a 1957 statement in which he said that "it was the opinion of our government that, on the question of boundary lines, demands made on the basis of formal treaties [concluded by former Chinese governments] should be respected according to general international practice."[10] This did not mean that the old boundary treaties would necessarily be permitted to function forever. On the contrary, the real expectation was that, at a propitious moment, the PRC and each of its neighbors would work out a mutually more satisfactory and precise graph of their joint periphery, as evidenced by the premier's accompanying comment that the admitted willingness of the Peking authorities to countenance the current situation on the PRC's frontiers "by no means excluded the seeking by two friendly countries of a settlement fair and reasonable for both sides through peaceful negotiations between their governments."[11] In short, the new regime was prepared in principle to tolerate the PRC's factual frontiers, but also anticipated their proximate segmentary resurvey at the diplomatic table.[12]

On neither count, then, did the Soviets appear to have grounds for worry about the inherent soundness of their extant frontier with the PRC.[13] To be sure, this does not imply that the Soviet title to the lands acquired from the Chinese empire over the centuries was unassailable. For that matter, if need be, the charge of "unequal treaties" could always be leveled to impugn the legitimacy of Soviet ownership of these territories. Again, though, the Chinese Communist government displayed no inclination to resort to that nihilistic weapon indiscriminately, so here, too, the Soviets saw no immediate cause for anxiety. The Mongolian occurrence may have provided food for thought in this connection, but Mongolia's experience was marked by two further qualifications, neither of which applied to the Soviet Union: Mongolia was a case sui generis since it had only recently seceded from China and the memory of their association was still fresh in everybody's mind; and, technically speaking, the MPR was a product of Kuomintang diplomacy and thus subject to the conditions enunciated in Article 55. Add to that the phenomenon of Peking's readiness, despite the complications just mentioned, to overlook these points and strike a bargain here essentially on Soviet terms, and the net result is a situation which must have afforded the Soviet government considerable satisfaction and relief for it let Moscow draw the conclusion that, if the tangled issue of Mongolia could be resolved with such ease, its own frontiers with the PRC, possessed of superior legal credentials by comparison, would a fortiori be spared vexing controversy.

THE TREATY OF FRIENDSHIP, ALLIANCE, AND MUTUAL AID, 1950

Nevertheless, even before the political friction between Moscow and Peking degenerated into an open split, the Chinese managed on four separate occasions to bring up the potentially explosive theme of boundary "corrections." The first, as previously indicated, dates from 1949 and involved Mongolia: in light of what has been said so far, the target picked is hardly surprising. The main outcome of the exchange of views that ensued has already been described and requires no elaboration. It is worth noting, however, that the incident may have had one other consequence, whose connection with these events is slightly more elusive, but nonetheless quite probable. At stake is the clause in the text of the Treaty of Friendship, Alliance, and Mutual Aid of February 14, 1950,[14] by which the Soviet Union and the PRC undertook to develop their reciprocal relations in accordance, inter alia, with the principle of "mutual respect for state sovereignty and territorial integrity."

The formula is common enough per se and would not warrant special attention if it were not for: 1) the subsequent disclosure that at the time these words were written into the agreement differences of opinion over territorial issues were being aired by the interested parties and the choice of vocabulary may have been fortuitous, but, on the other hand, may equally have reflected the tensions generated by this divergence of opinion; and, 2) repeated subsequent invocation of this passage by various Soviet sources in conjunction with discussions of the ongoing border dispute between the Soviet Union and the PRC as though the artifact had been designed for this specific contingency, an item which raises the distinct possibility that indeed it was. Assuming the featured expression had a definite purpose, the question remains as to which side originated it and engineered its inclusion in the final version of the document.

The initial tendency is to attribute the stratagem to the PRC, based on the instinctual feeling that China, having lost territory in the past, would now have most to gain by insisting on strict observance of the norm of territorial integrity as a way of dramatizing its cause, as a bar to further encroachments on its domain, or as a preliminary step in an attempt to set the stage for recouping at least a portion of the ceded lands. It must be admitted, however, that, taken at face value, the proposition is utterly neutral: the phraseology will serve a "revisionist" thesis just as it will support a defense of the status quo. Coupled with the fact that Soviet spokesmen have relied with increasing frequency on this pronouncement to make the point that the PRC had thereby formally recognized the operative frontiers between the two countries and from then on was legally bound to maintain the existing boundary line and to refrain from disturbing the regime established on the state border, the interpretation that the Soviet Union may have been the architect of the scheme recommends itself with some force.[15] Besides, nothing in the record says that both signatories did not seek to insert this proviso, each for reasons of its own which did not match the motives of the other partner, except that these latent contradictions were left unarticulated at the time in expectation perhaps that they might be unveiled with greater profit at a future date.

THE SINO-SOVIET DISCUSSIONS OF 1954

The next round took place at the private Sino-Soviet discussions in Peking in 1954, and once again the bone of contention turned out to be Mongolia. The published accounts of what transpired during this second encounter differ, since the parties recall the event in order to accuse each other of bad faith or worse. To hear Peking tell the story, "according to the Yalta agreement, the Soviet Union, under the pretext of guaranteeing the independence of Mongolia, has actually placed that country under its domination. . . . In 1954, when Khrushchev and Bulganin came to China, we raised this question,

BACKGROUND 7

but they refused to talk to us."[16] In rebuttal, the Soviets contend that:

> They [the Chinese leaders] would like to deprive the MPR of independence and make it a Chinese province. It was precisely on this that the PRC leaders proposed the "reaching of agreement" to N. S. Khrushchev and other Soviet comrades during their visit to Peking in 1954. N. S. Khrushchev naturally refused to discuss this question and told the Chinese leaders that the destiny of the Mongolian people was determined not in Peking and not in Moscow but in Ulan-Bator, that the question of Mongolia's statehood could be settled only by the country's working people themselves and by nobody else.[17]

Soviet commentators paint the picture in even more ominous colors, charging that Mao Tse-tung repeated his earlier (1949) performance and "confronted the Soviet leadership with the 'problem' of merging the MPR with China" or, as he himself later allegedly informed a visiting group of Japanese socialists, that he had "demanded of them [the Soviet leaders] the return of Outer Mongolia, but they refused."[18]

The timing of the episode is suggestive, for it coincides with the end of Soviet influence in Sinkiang. Having reasserted their role in various vital sectors of the region's economy long monopolized by the Soviets, the Chinese Communists in four brief years consummated their reversion to Peking's sole control. Khrushchev's trip to the PRC in 1954 to all intents and purposes marked the close of an epoch as, with his acquiescence in the dissolution of the Sino-Soviet joint stock corporations, the curtain rang down on the last remainders of the once preponderant Soviet "presence" in this corner of Inner Asia. With that as an example, one can easily imagine the Chinese next pressing the Soviets to relax their grip on Mongolia and arrive at a modus vivendi that would give the Chinese an equal voice in Mongolian affairs, in the hope that ultimately Mongolia, just as Sinkiang previously, would slip out of the Soviet orbit and gravitate toward the PRC. There is little doubt that PRC aspirations ran in the direction of the imminent "voluntary return" of Mongolia to its traditional association with the Chinese nation. After all, as everyone is fond of pointing out, back in 1936, Mao, not noted for a short memory, had explained to Edgar Snow that "when the people's revolution has been victorious in China, the Outer Mongolian republic will automatically become part of the Chinese federation, at their own will."[19]

Thus, what the Chinese probably wanted was a fair share in the management of Mongolia and a chance to convert the Mongols to the idea of a "free reunion" of their country with the Chinese Motherland. The Soviets, at a guess, wished to preserve Mongolia's strong ties

with Moscow and blocked the Chinese bid for a deal by appealing to
Mongolia's sovereignty, which on balance spelled the maintenance of
the existing system, together with its pro-Soviet orientation. Doubtless, neither side was in this instance guilty of the horrible designs
the other was later to impute to it: the Soviets did not "occupy" Mongolia and insist on perpetuating their hegemony over the area; conversely, the Chinese did not try to persuade the Soviets to consent to
a unilateral incorporation of Mongolia into the PRC domain. More
subtle tactics were employed by both to promote their local ambitions,
nicely cloaked behind technical talk of border rectifications.

A decade elapsed before any of this information saw the light of
day. However, as in 1949, an echo of the polemic found its way into
the tenor of the document which summed up the results of the meeting.
In effect, the Joint Declaration on Various Questions concerning the
International Situation, released at the closing session on October 12,
1954,[20] contained a paragraph in which the respective governments
stipulated that the friendly relations already in existence between the
two countries would "be the basis for further cooperation between
them in accordance with the principles of equality, mutual benefit,
and mutual respect for sovereignty and territorial integrity." This
triad has been correctly identified as a Mao foreign policy prop[21]
and the reference to territorial integrity in the present context clearly
hints at the live nature and continued importance of the subject as a
topic of diplomatic business between Moscow and Peking. From this
piece of indirect evidence alone, one would have ample reason to conclude that the question of territorial "adjustments" did feature on the
conference agenda. A corollary implication is that the initiative to
have the final communique reaffirm both signatories' adherence to
the principle of territorial integrity emanated from the Chinese side.
(The impression is strengthened by the fact that during this period
PRC legal analysts regularly cited respect for territorial integrity
among the normative desiderata applicable to relations between all
states, including "socialist" states. By contrast, their Soviet counterparts then insisted that "socialist" states dealt with one another pursuant to the canon of "socialist internationalism" which made no
mention of "territorial integrity" ostensibly because under the code
of conduct of the "socialist commonwealth" such a reminder was
superfluous.)

As previously suggested, however, even though the Chinese may
in practice have been responsible for the allusion to "territorial
integrity" in this case, the Soviets could also have been quite capable
of doing so entirely on their own or should have had no insuperable
objections to going along with the proposal, if it turned out that the
idea did originate with the Chinese. A curt nod in the general direction
of "territorial integrity," without spelling out what was meant by the

BACKGROUND 9

gesture, not only could not hurt the Soviet Union's cause, but indeed could improve its bargaining position by giving Moscow an excuse to claim that the formula was aimed at guaranteeing the inviolability of the current frontier arrangements. Soviet lawyers have since taken exactly that tack and appealed, inter alia, to the pertinent language of the 1954 communique in support of their argument.[22]

THE SINO-SOVIET DISCUSSIONS OF 1957

Of the third skirmish, only the PRC's version is available, and this account, too, is retrospective. "At the interview with Premier Khrushchev in January 1957," Chou En-lai is quoted as saying, "I requested that the USSR make proper arrangements for the territorial issues covering Japan, China, the Middle East, and the Eastern European countries including Finland. I could not get a satisfactory answer from him then, but the announcement of the issue was kept secret because the Sino-Soviet dispute was not public at the time."[23] Not much can be gleaned from this cryptic statement, but the highly unusual circumstances in which the information was "leaked" offer some useful clues on what might have prompted the PRC's latest bid to engage the Soviets in a discussion over territorial matters. In effect, Chou En-lai's visit to Moscow followed upon his tour of Eastern Europe ostensibly launched in an attempt to heal the widening rift between the Soviet Union and the neighboring Communist regimes in the wake of the Polish and Hungarian events. Outwardly playing the part of neutral moderator and urging both sides to tone down their demands and settle their quarrels amicably, he meanwhile assiduously cultivated in his audiences the image of the PRC as an impartial arbiter on the correct terms of association between "proletarian nations" and an authority on the etiquette of state conduct within the self-styled "socialist commonwealth," with judicious praise and criticism for everybody involved.

The East Europeans were counseled not to indulge in Russian baiting and not to push the Kremlin to where it might lose patience and turn violent, applauded for their awareness of the "activities and danger of reactionary elements" in their midst, and pressed to eradicate these "enemies" ruthlessly. And, in the next breath, the Soviet leaders were chided, by inference, for neglecting "the principle of equality among nations in their mutual relations," warned that "such a mistake, by nature, is the error of bourgeois chauvinism," that, particularly when committed by a big country, it "inevitably results in serious damage to the solidarity and common cause of the socialist countries," and, by example, exhorted to eternal vigilance "to prevent the error of big nation chauvinism in relations with socialist countries and others."[24]

In short, with the Soviets in disarray, the Chinese seized the opportunity to pose simultaneously as champions of the "just aspirations" of the smaller Communist states vis-a-vis the Soviet colossus and staunch defenders of the "integral unity of the socialist camp." Presumably, for these services, Moscow would be heavily indebted to Peking for helping restore order and discipline in the Soviet Union's front yard, the East European states would feel grateful to it for espousing their cause against unreasonable Soviet pretensions, and, as a consequence, the PRC's influence in the region would be substantially enhanced. Whether or not the Chinese really fancied themselves in the role of official partner of the Russians in setting the general policy in Communist East Europe is hard to tell. Such calculations do not lie beyond the realm of credibility. At any rate, whatever their ulterior objectives, the Chinese at this point did not hesitate to lecture their "Western allies" on the accepted norms of international "socialist" behavior or recommend to them specific solutions for their present difficulties.

No conflicting territorial claims were publicly aired at this stage. The atmosphere was sufficiently volatile without looking for extra aggravations, but the Russians themselves had, all too unwittingly, introduced the subject, at least in a manner of speaking, when they issued the famous "Declaration of the Foundations of Development and Further Consolidation of Friendship and Cooperation between the Soviety Union and Other Socialist States" of October 30, 1956.[25] Therein Moscow took the unprecedented step of openly endorsing the proposition that "the countries of the great commonwealth of socialist nations can build their relations only on the principle of full equality, respect for territorial integrity, state independence and sovereignty, and noninterference in one another's domestic affairs." The Chinese were quick to pick up the item and the PRC government's statement of November 1, 1956, in response to the Soviet pronouncement, put stronger emphasis on that theme than had the Soviets. For Peking, "mutual relations between socialist countries all the more so should be established on the basis of these five principles," since "only in this way are the socialist countries able to achieve genuine fraternal friendship and solidarity. . . ."[26]

The explicit mention of "respect for territorial integrity" in the Kremlin's manifesto (and, remember, in this case the Soviet authorities <u>unilaterally</u> decided to inject this relatively unorthodox formula into the bylaws of the "socialist international community"), prominently echoed in the Chinese document, may very well have inspired the PRC's delegation to broach here the question of possible frontier "adjustments" by the Soviet Union in favor of several of the surrounding states. One can readily imagine Chou En-lai suggesting to Khrushchev that, if the modus vivendi between the Soviet Union and

BACKGROUND 11

its confederates were to be thoroughly overhauled, a few territorial concessions to members of the inner family, the PRC included, might be a tangible method of demonstrating the new approach and the most effective means of cementing the unity of the "socialist" world. Furthermore, as long as the current Soviet leadership had recognized the value of the "neutralist" countries and was seeking appropriate ways of expressing its support for them and of convincing other peoples to embrace that attitude, suitable border compromises for the benefit of Finland, Japan, and various lands in the Middle East might offer the best proof of its appreciation for their contribution to international diplomacy.

It is most unlikely that Chou En-lai ever nurtured hopes of detaching large chunks of peripheral Soviet territory and parceling them out among the interested contiguous states or would even have approved then of any scheme of the sort. What he probably did contemplate was a process whereby the Soviet Union would negotiate afresh with its neighbors on where their respective boundary lines ought to run, show a spirit of conciliation, and subscribe to technical changes in the corresponding section of the border to accommodate the legitimate grievances of the other side. True, the Soviet Union would stand to lose a bit of acreage as a result; in return, though, it would gain frontiers guaranteed by ironclad treaties concluded between equals. Moscow was not, one can safely assume, asked to act as a voluntary donor, nor to prove that it was occasionally capable of munificence just because it chose to, since that would smack of patronage, but to deal with the matter on a business plane, trading some space for good will, a patch of ground for political advantages accruing from increased confidence, esteem, and loyalty on the part of those handled with such sympathy and understanding.

Not surprisingly, the Soviets betrayed little enthusiasm for their chief ally's undisguised inclination to sound generous with Soviet soil. Nevertheless, the joint Soviet-Chinese declaration issued to commemorate Chou En-lai's stay in the Soviet Union,[27] duly repeated the earlier reference to relations between "fraternal peoples" resting on the so-called "Five Principles," one element of which, of course, was "respect for territorial integrity." The same scenario may fit this episode as was previously sketched to explain comparable phenomena in 1950 and 1954. To add continuity to the experience, Soviet legal spokesmen have since bracketed the 1957 mention of the concept of territorial integrity together with the 1950 and 1954 examples to back their claim that the formula was plainly intended to perpetuate the status quo on the Sino-Soviet frontier and to record that neither party harbored any "revisionist" thoughts on that score.[28]

Whatever the Soviet government's motives in letting itself be publicly indentified with the use of such language on these four occasions in a context involving the enunciation of standards applicable to relations among "socialist" states, the dominant impression is that the Soviets never felt quite comfortable cast in that role. This malaise may be the reason why they then suddenly put an end to the practice and dropped the article from the official script. After all, to capture the essence of the intramural activities of the "socialist" community, the Soviets have always deemed "socialist internationalism" a more suitable term of art than "peaceful coexistence" and they forthwith returned to their first choice. In addition, it may well be that the PRC's insistence on dredging up the territorial issue finally convinced the Soviets that continued accent on the theme of territorial integrity in Sino-Soviet diplomatic documents might encourage the Chinese to persevere in this endeavor and that it would be better all around if the subject were withdrawn from circulation, which they unobtrusively proceeded to do.

BORDER CORRECTIONS PROBE—
BUZ-AIGYR, 1960

The fourth probe about border corrections dates from 1960, when Chou En-lai "at a press conference in Katmandu in Nepal on April 28. . . was asked whether there were any 'unestablished sections on the Soviet-Chinese frontiers' and he replied: 'There are insignificant discrepancies in the maps, easy to solve peacefully'."[29] Apparently, the by-play had a private sequel: Peking subsequently disclosed that "on August 22 and September 21, 1960, the Chinese Government took the initiative in proposing to the Soviet Government that negotiations be held" on the topic of a comprehensive boundary settlement.[30] As far as is known, nothing came of these overtures either. Not to be outdone, Soviet sources claimed that the government of the Soviet Union repeatedly took the initiative in proposing that consultations be held on the question of precisely identifying the line of the Soviet-Chinese frontier in particular sectors and that efforts to get the Chinese to discuss the project had started already back in 1960.[31]

What impelled the Soviet authorities to take such a step at that time has yet to be explained, but they may have been reacting to something that reportedly had just occurred and which could have precipitated this type of response. Nineteen-sixty is recalled in Soviet literature as the year which witnessed the first Sino-Soviet border incident, allegedly provoked that summer by the PRC in the vicinity of Buz-Aigyr (in the Tien Shan mountain range along the boundary with Sinkiang) when more than a hundred Chinese cattleherders deliberately violated the state frontier of the Soviet

BACKGROUND 13

Union and penetrated deep into Soviet territory. Despite the demands of the Soviet frontier guards, these people would not return to the PRC and persisted in their refusal even after winter had set in, compelling the Soviet authorities to provide them with the necessary supplies. Interrogation by the frontier guards as to why they would still not go back when they had run out of fodder for their animals elicited from the chairman of a people's commune who was a member of the group the admission that the crossing had been effected on the direct orders of the PRC administration and that they were afraid to head for home without their superiors' permission.[32]

The account of what followed is even more interesting and, according to the Soviets, the Chinese performance here put a completely new slant on their intentions in this area. For, if Soviet spokesmen are to be believed, "in the course of diplomatic exchanges in connection with this incident, the Chinese government expressed the view that the ownership of the territory was questionable and it would be expedient to hold consultations on the boundary line in the region of Buz-Aigyr." However, they added, the PRC authorities "subsequently avoided holding such consultations although the Soviet side had agreed to the proposal."[33] Another Soviet version credits settlement of the incident to the "friendly and patient position of the government of the USSR" in that:

> The Ministry of Foreign Affairs of the PRC, striving to exculpate the violators of the frontier, declared that it was necessary to conduct consultations to resolve the disputed questions. It argued as though certain segments of the frontier "are not established" and the "established portion also was not inspected by the Chinese and Soviet sides after the creation of the PRC." In the Soviet note, handed to the Ministry of Foreign Affairs of the PRC on October 29, 1960, it was stated that the government of the USSR does not object to friendly consultations through diplomatic channels, if the PRC should so insist. But it does not consider debatable the question of the ownership by the USSR of the area north of the Buz-Aigyr pass.[34]

One thing seems clear from all this and that is that no matter what merit Moscow's "friendly and patient position" may have had in ending the affair, its attitude did not achieve a "settlement," except in the sense that the Chinese eventually dropped their bid. In light of the fact that the Chinese had contested title to the land itself and the Soviets had rejected that contention out of hand and appeared prepared only to discuss the fixing of the extant boundary line in situ, negotiations were apt to be in vain anyway for lack of a common focus or theme. Nevertheless, the failure of the Chinese even to try to use the diplomatic process to air their case or otherwise articulate grounds for a substantive claim is a significant aspect of the record suggesting a definite modus operandi in which the fate of the Buz-Aigyr morsel featured as a symbol or a symptom for ulterior purposes rather than as a cause of concern for its own sake.

It is important to note that already before that some problems had been encountered on the Sino-Soviet frontier. Soviet sources acknowledge that

> as far back as 1956-1959 Soviet frontier guards had repeatedly pointed out to the Chinese authorities that there were instances of Chinese citizens violating the border. The border authorities of both parties settled these questions in a businesslike atmosphere and no misunderstanding requiring the interference of central authorities arose.

They also add that:

> Guided by the interests of further consolidating good-neighborly relations with the PRC, the Soviet Union at the time offered to conclude a treaty with the PRC, as well as with other countries, on the regulation of the boundary line and on settling border questions by mutual agreement. But the Chinese side evaded the discussion of such a proposal.[35]

The Buz-Aigyr affair, then, was qualitatively different from this earlier spate of border "irregularities" in that the Soviets perceived it as having been deliberately staged at the instigation of the PRC government: they also perceived that the problem could not be settled at the local level and that PRC officialdom had used the occasion to formulate a territorial claim against the Soviet Union and avoided being drawn into negotiations to deal with the issue. An adversary situation had thus been created which, the Soviets said, signaled the beginning of a new phase in Sino-Soviet border relations and ushered in a period marked by a PRC policy of conscious and systematic violation of the frontier between the two countries. In 1961-62, by Moscow's count, several thousand cases of infringement of the boundary line by the Chinese had been registered.[36]

BACKGROUND 15

Since all this information was released only in the last few years, one must be aware of the possibility that the script has been doctored to take full advantage of the wisdom of hindsight and adapt the evidence to fit current exigencies based on the history of intervening events. Making due allowance for this phenomenon, an attempt to reconstruct a less partisan version of the record may prove a worthwhile enterprise by offering a viable alternative interpretation of essentially the same set of data and developing a perspective that might come nearer reflecting what actually did happen in this instance.

First, the duration and frequency of border incidents in Sino-Soviet relations, coupled with the casual manner in which these episodes were treated prior to 1960, tend to suggest that something about the very nature of the boundary line lent itself to the persistence and proliferation of cases of "trespass." As outside observers have long remarked and the Chinese have taken pains to emphasize during the past decade, the frontier is indeed full of blank spots and ambiguous stretches which are peculiarly prone to engender controversy on where the dividing line is supposed to run.

Second, the customs and life style of the native population evince little sympathy and respect for artificial barriers and traditionally put no premium on deference to paper injunctions designed to restrict the free movement of local nomadic tribes and their herds and flocks. This attitude was especially prevalent on the outer rim of Sinkiang where Buz-Aigyr is located.

Third, in an objective sense, the pre- and post-1960 conditions along portions of the Sino-Soviet frontier with respect to so-called border intrusions were probably much the same. Border "violations" occurred regularly in the period of 1956-59, and yet Soviet spokesmen still remember that first decade as a time when friendship and good-neighborliness reigned on the Sino-Soviet frontier. Broad ties were maintained between the populations of the border zone, active trade developed, cultural exchanges were organized, economic projects were jointly undertaken, mutual assistance was routinely extended, and cooperation was arranged to combat natural disasters. The Soviet authorities permitted the Chinese population to mow hay, cut wood, catch fish, and engage in similar quotidian activities in several sections of Soviet territory. Soviet and Chinese frontier guards established close comradely contacts, and questions which arose on the border were always handled in an atmosphere of mutual understanding and propriety.[37]

The particle which seems to have changed in 1960, then, was the psychological climate. Relations between the Soviet Union and the PRC had meanwhile soured and this affected the parties' reflexes though the stimuli remained virtually identical. (Note that even with the bitterness born of the 1969 bloodshed, Soviet official sources still go no further than to charge the PRC in the early 1960s with "small, insignificant violations of the existing border regime, committed as a rule by the civilian population," except to say that "in separate sectors Chinese servicemen attempted to violate openly the state border of the Soviet Union.")[38] Nevertheless, what had been a nuisance henceforth became a provocation, what had been viewed in the past as innocent error was presently perceived as premeditated malice, every common infringement of the boundary line turned into a deliberate violation. Without a doubt, numerous cases outwardly resembling Buz-Aigyr had occurred earlier without qualifying as a cause célèbre simply due to the absence of will or desire on either side to make a big issue over a minor item.

Fourth, if, as one suspects, the site of the encounter did lie in an area where the precise contour of the boundary line was uncertain, the whole thing boils down to the size of a very ordinary and comparatively trivial border conflict. This is not an outgrowth of the grand territorial dispute foreshadowed by the 1949, 1954 and 1957 experiences, the subject of which was the configuration of the PRC's entire northern perimeter or major segments thereof and the status of large pieces of adjoining territory, but an average disagreement over a concrete parcel of land (petty stuff befitting the casual vein of Chou En-lai's impromptu remarks at Katmandu). The former theme conjured up visions of a "comprehensive boundary settlement," the latter occasion merely evoked prospects of a standard exercise in physical redemarcation on a local scale.

Indeed, the only real distinction between the Buz-Aigyr affair and many other analogous incidents elsewhere on the Sino-Soviet frontier, both before and after, was that the Chinese chose on this occasion to file a claim to a particular bit of terrain and to assert that the proper position of the boundary line in this area should be ascertained, whereas hitherto they had silently acquiesced in a succession of ad hoc solutions which in practice had left the status quo intact and never looked into the legal validity of the current modus vivendi. The latest shift in tactics effectively transformed a factual phenomenon into a juridical equation. The question that remains unanswered, of course, is whether the Chinese deliberately staged the "confrontation" in the manner described by the Soviets in order to dramatize their contention that the present state of the Sino-Soviet frontier was unsatisfactory and thus hoped to prod the Soviets into subscribing to the Chinese proposal that they seek a comprehensive boundary settlement or that they simply picked a convenient opportunity—a routine specimen of a contested border crossing—to try to achieve that end.

CONCLUSIONS

The preceding discussion represents the sum total of the hard data on concrete Sino-Soviet discussions that developed during this period on the subject of frontiers. The fund of available information is meager; yet, the record of these early years already contained the germs of subsequent events. To begin with, in all cases the initiative for bringing up the problem of frontier revisions emanated from the Chinese; they are the ones who seemed to show an intense interest in talking about the issue, whereas the Soviets invariably shied away from the topic. Then, if statements about past events can be trusted and the record has not been retroactively cosmetized to serve latter-day needs, a neat dichotomy soon emerged between the respective focus of Chinese and Soviet efforts in this domain: the Chinese wanted the agenda to feature all aspects of the border problem or at least its most important components and they refused to get involved in a round of piecemeal "rectifications" of individual stretches of the frontier; by contrast, the Soviets would have no truck with anything that smacked of a substantive review of the status of the existing frontiers and advocated instead limited adjustments in appropriate sections of the de facto boundary line to eliminate immediate causes of friction or conflict. Each party has since stuck to that position with rare consistency. Under the circumstances, it is also quite understandable why the Chinese were less than enthusiastic about the Soviet idea of a bilateral treaty on the regulation of the boundary line and the settlement of border questions by mutual agreement: in practical terms, such an accord would have operated to freeze the status quo and render more difficult the task of the side hoping to effect changes in the old regime for its own benefit.

Next, although Peking's spokesmen had attempted to engage the Soviets in serious conversation on the territorial theme, their efforts were not made public. Even if the request to keep the matter quiet is attributed to the Kremlin, the Chinese gave their consent with no sign of hesitation and for a long time faithfully abided by the compact. The "indiscretion" at Katmandu is an exception to the rule, but one has reason to believe that what happened on this occasion was not part of the original script, for Chinese sources now describe the episode as having been triggered by "the provocative question of an American correspondent."[39] Still, for a statement voiced in a relatively open forum, it went virtually unheeded. More important, Chou's answer was couched in a tone so deprecatory as to make the issue sound almost trivial. The three previous bids to explore the matter further with the Soviets were pursued in strict confidence and only nine years later did a bare trickle of information on two of these ventures leak out. In fact, what little is known of the 1949 episode comes exclusively from Soviet writings and the same is true as regards news of the first bona fide Sino-Soviet border "conflict" at Buz-Aigyr. Again, the initial spell of silence which surrounded these events may have been due to Moscow's desire not to advertise these awkward developments abroad, a wish which the Chinese were willing to observe and did until the Soviets themselves lifted the veil of secrecy from both incidents.

Finally, while the Chinese evidently felt quite free to raise the territorial question at opportune moments, they never formulated fixed demands or advanced specific claims in that connection, but dealt just in generalities. Even more significant, of the four documented instances when the subject was broached in the privacy of Sino-Soviet diplomatic discussions, only two involved the Soviet Union directly, —in 1957 and 1960 (Katmandu). In both 1949 and 1954, Mongolia's fate was at stake and the Soviet Union appeared on the scene solely in its capacity as Mongolia's protector: its home ground, as far as one can tell, did not star as a bone of contention in either case. And, although the Buz-Aigyr affair does represent a concrete border conflict (as distinct from a panoramic territorial dispute), the critical factor is that here, too, no catalogue of detailed grievances or list of sought for changes was forthcoming and yet the situation per se warranted (indeed, perhaps dictated) a technical approach par excellence, geared to explicitly identifying and defining the problems to be solved. The inference is that while the Buz-Aigyr business was a separate item and severable from the territorial phenomenon, the Chinese were determined to link the two elements and through this medium harness the potency of local border tensions to the job of extracting a global frontier accommodation (without, in the process, necessarily sacrificing the corollary goal of securing favorable on-the-spot border "corrections"). To play that game successfully, the border issue could not be allowed to acquire an independent existence, for then it might have proved susceptible to ad hoc treatment and failed as an ancillary weapon in the territorial context, and an easy way of avoiding that contingency was by not volunteering any vital statistics concerning the purported claim and keeping the relevant contextual format as vague as possible.

A distinctive pattern thus emerged. The Chinese tendered clear notice to their Soviet associates that they viewed the frontier problem as a live issue. However, they also thought of it as a private affair, best left unadvertised, and throughout treated it as a piece of business which, albeit deserving of attention, conveyed no sense of imminent crisis. Moreover, Peking consistently advocated a negotiated settlement, without prejudging either the character or the extent of the territorial concessions which the Soviets might eventually

BACKGROUND   19

decide to grant as a result of such diplomatic pourparlers, so that, by the looks of it, the actual procedure perhaps counted more than the substantive terms of any particular bargain struck by the parties. By contrast, the Soviets simply refused to debate the topic and, at the very most, expressed a readiness to consider resurveying and marking certain narrow segments of the border where the boundary line obviously stood in urgent need of retracing.

The incidental details likewise fitted neatly into the assembled mosaic. For instance, much has been made of the fact that the Chinese Communists have on various occasions published maps in which vast tracts of land around the PRC's rim, including portions of the Soviet Union, were designated as "lost territories."[40] The most famous episode entailed a map featured in a history text printed in Peking in 1953 (2d ed., 1954)[41] purporting to identify all the nearby areas that once "belonged" to China and of which it was despoiled in the last century by the "imperialist powers," Russia among them. The technique is not new, of course, and maps have often served in the past as a convenient method of airing territorial claims and, at the same time, "scientifically proving" the validity of the rights being asserted. The trouble in this case is that there is no evidence that the Chinese Communist regime ever attempted to use the material in this manner.

First, an obscure volume issued in the Chinese language was hardly a suitable vehicle for such purposes, for if the intention was to let the adversary know how Peking felt about the profile of their common border, the chances of that aim being duly accomplished through this medium were poor. Next, the available data tend to indicate that while the authorities did not prevent foreigners living in the PRC from picking up copies of the book in question, they made no positive efforts to disseminate it abroad. Indeed, to believe a latter-day Soviet account frankly hostile to the Chinese and calculated to put Chinese conduct in the worst possible light, allegedly "the Chinese leaders...for a time kept such books and maps secret from foreigners." True or not, ten years elapsed before Moscow suddenly woke up to the "vital importance" of the message it now discovered in the map.[42]

On balance, perhaps the most telling evidence against Soviet attempts to attribute in retrospect a sinister quality to these so-called exercises in "cartographic aggression" was the Soviet government's failure during all this time to protest against the Chinese practice. Even if the PRC officialdom did restrict the circulation of the 1954 volume and others like it, several neighbors of the PRC apparently managed to learn of these activities and, according to the Soviets, they forthwith filed formal protests with Peking on the subject. It is hard to believe that the Soviets were less well-informed on that score and yet Soviet sources offer no indication that Moscow ever bothered then to register a complaint with Peking concerning the matter, a striking omission which prompts the conclusion that, while the existence of such maps was almost certainly no mystery to the men in the Kremlin, nobody there paid much attention to the item in those days.[43]

In short, nothing in the historical record substantiates the charge either that Peking thus counted on laying the groundwork for challenging the Soviet Union's legal title to a number of regions contiguous to Chinese soil or that the Soviet authorities (in contrast to other neighbors of China who shared the experience) currently saw the Chinese moves in that light. Furthermore, if that is what the Chinese leadership had in mind, it plainly plumped for a self-defeating procedure to attain this objective. To be sure, rank ineptitude is not ruled out, but even in that respect the caliber of Peking's performance would strain credibility. A more intelligent conclusion would be to accept the spectacle at face value—as a relatively innocuous display of patriotic bombast. In that context, the Chinese readiness in 1963, when pressed to account for this phenomenon, simply to repudiate the map as though dismissing a petty detail made a lot of sense.

Admittedly, a year later at the 1964 trade fair in Mexico City, the Communist Chinese are said to have distributed a booklet containing a map that pictured the Soviet Union's Maritime Provinces as part of the PRC.[44] On closer look, though, the circumstances of the occurrence would seem to support, not deny, the points previously made. Except for the novelty that the Chinese chose to air their views in public (a step which recalls the way in which the rest of the Sino-Soviet polemic had gradually emerged into the open), both the place and the modus operandi were utterly inappropriate for framing a legal argument for the PRC's pretensions to territory currently owned by the Soviets. Rather, the physical setting hints at a very different explanation. Moscow and Peking were then freely vying for the favor of the Latin Americans and under those conditions spreading a diagram of the sort suited the nature of the game: at a single stroke, the Soviets were portrayed as usurpers of foreign soil. The Latin Americans remembered how they themselves suffered from the depredations of U.S. imperialism, and, in their eyes, the Soviets and the Americans were lumped together under the label of arrogant great powers preying on their weaker neighbors, while the Chinese were perceived as fellow victims of that greed. In sum, it all amounted to a skillful political maneuver, but came nowhere near constituting any kind of a legal case. In fact, even on a strictly political plane, the gesture rated as little more than a slight poke in the psyche, enough to annoy the Soviets, but not capable of causing any real damage.

Maps on which the track of the frontier deviates from the profile forged by applicable treaties or fixed by long usage or sections of the boundary line that are marked "undetermined" represent a different and more serious business. They may, and often do, reflect a practical diplomatic problem stemming from a concrete divergence of opinion over rights of possession of particular pieces of land or even sizeable expanses of terrain in which an alternate version of the border or the contention that the local boundary line has never been properly established serves notice of a competing claim. Hence, the significance of the conspicuous absence of this key element in the Sino-Soviet case can hardly be exaggerated. Soviet sources, which no longer hesitate to accuse the Chinese of waging systematic "cartographic aggression" and, in a number of instances, recklessly escalating these "hostilities" to the level of "cartographic war,"[45] can only cite a 1950 wall map of the PRC in which segments of the PRC's frontier in the Pamirs were described as "undetermined" as a sample of such behavior which affected the Soviet Union.[46] And again, while Soviet scribes take pleasure in pointing out that most of the PRC's other neighbors responded to this and similar examples of Peking's "provocative conduct" by addressing official protests to the Chinese authorities, none mentions that the Soviet government resorted to comparable measures. This diplomatic silence, in turn, adds to the impression that either that breed of trouble did not loom large on the Sino-Soviet horizon or that it was not taken to heart by the Soviets and the Chinese, especially the Soviets; or perhaps both factors were operating.

This still leaves the problem of whether the Chinese regime was not deliberately trying to manufacture a "revisionist mood" at home by sanctioning the insertion of "inflammatory" items in a set of popular textbooks. The suggestion here is that the chart was not earmarked primarily for foreign consumption nor posted as a sign of an impending PRC drive to "recover territories amputated from the mother country," but injected into the mass educational system in order to create a propitious climate of opinion preparatory to launching a diplomatic offensive to wrest drastic territorial concessions from adjoining nations. The tactic is an old one and has much to recommend it. However, its effectiveness largely hinges on the leadership's ability and willingness to mount a vocal popular campaign to dramatize and magnify the issue and soften up the intended target. That cardinal element was precisely what was lacking from the mainland scene.[47] On the contrary, from the impression gathered by most outside observers, the experiment was apparently motivated by the same sober wish to cultivate in the younger generation pride in their land's glorious heritage which is often encountered elsewhere and which, in virtually identical guise, was standard fare in the school curricula under the previous

Chinese administrations.[48] Use of the theme of a nation's heroic past to stimulate "love of country" is quite a different matter from consciously exploiting it to promote "revanchist" schemes. True enough, one sometimes degenerates into the other, so the problem must be tackled with due caution. However, as yet, no clues have been forthcoming of a foreseeable shift on this front from an attitude of perhaps prickly, albeit essentially still defensive, nationalism to a policy of militant and expansion-minded irredentism. The distance between the two positions is considerable, and there is nothing to indicate that the present PRC leadership is poised to take the dangerous leap.

Actually, the best evidence in support of this strand of analysis may be found in the documented record of the public treatment accorded in Communist China in those days to the early history of Russo-Chinese competition over border districts. Thus, a thorough survey of pre-1962 Communist Chinese literature aimed at establishing the accepted instructional approach to the sensitive topic of the methods by which Russia managed to acquire the Maritime Provinces reports that "the concise histories of China which had been published on the mainland since the beginning of the Communist regime seldom specifically mention Russian expansion into the Maritime territory. Even when such reference is included, efforts are made to avoid elaboration of the Russian episode. Consequently, especially in the books intended for mass consumption, such important events as the conclusion of the Chinese-Russian Treaties of Aigun, Tientsin, and Peking have simply been omitted."[49] "Advanced academic treatises," judging by this study, have been less reticent in painting an accurate picture of Russian ambitions in this sector and the stratagems used to realize Russia's goals. On balance, though, the most striking feature here was the obvious

> disparity of presentation of Russian activities in the Maritime territory between the Chinese Communist accounts intended for mass consumption and those of a more scholarly nature. In the former case, the general policy would seem to be one of avoiding mention of the episodes of Russian expansion on the grounds that this is remote in terms of time, having occurred a century ago, and also in terms of space. Russian activities in the Maritime territory were far removed from the center of activities in China and consequently of little concern to the masses in their daily life. The Chinese Communist historians can gloss over these incidents on the safe grounds that this is the proper historical perspective and

BACKGROUND 23

>position for the events. At the same time, they can be
>sure of avoiding any unnecessary irritation to their
>present-day Soviet ally. This is entirely in keeping with
>the great emphasis placed on proletarian internationalism.
>It is also a means to eliminate any possible grounds for
>sentiments of great-nation chauvinism or small-nation
>narrow nationalism in Sino-Soviet relations.[50]

A second experience conveyed the same desire for discreet mutual accommodation. In this instance, a newspaper story concerning certain cartographic discrepancies between Soviet and Chinese versions of the exact location of the PRC's boundary line with the Soviet Union, Mongolia, and Afghanistan dwelled on the likely diplomatic implications of these developments in the context of the widening ideological rift, but conceded that:

>as Western mapmakers and political experts puzzle over
>these map differences, there is no indication that either
>the Soviet Union or Communist China is concerned about
>the matter. Except for the cartographic evidence, neither
>side appears to discuss the matter in its official publica-
>tions.[51]

Finally, the various policy declarations issued in that period dealing with the status of the PRC's frontiers also followed this set pattern. Typical, for instance, were Chou En-lai's remarks at the Bandung Conference to the effect that:

>With some of these countries [possessing common
>borders with the PRC] we have not yet finally fixed our
>border line and we are ready to do so with our neigh-
>boring countries. But before doing so, we are willing
>to maintain the present situation by acknowledging
>that those parts of our border are parts which are
>undetermined. We are ready to restrain our Govern-
>ment and people from crossing even one step across
>our border. If such things should happen, we would
>like to admit our mistake. As the determination of
>common borders which we are going to undertake
>with our neighboring countries, we shall use only
>peaceful means and we shall not permit any other
>kinds of method. In no case shall we change this.[52]

Then, on October 1, 1959, Chou, in talking about the number of frontiers with other nations that had not been demarcated, reportedly reiterated that the PRC had claims on all of them and that the countries involved comprised the Soviet Union, Mongolia, Pakistan, North Korea, North Vietnam, Burma, and Nepal, but again did not embroider on his statement. More to the point, during the Hundred Flowers interlude in 1957, several prominent Chinese asserted that they saw little to choose between tsarist and Soviet imperialism or, the Soviets say, even spread overt "territorial demands" against the Soviet Union, and the Party leadership in Peking quickly moved to suppress these heretical views.[53]

SUMMARY

In summary, prior to 1963, the Communist Chinese hierarchy lost no opportunity to remind the states abutting on the PRC that frontier questions still remained open. In the process, it took good care not to sound either belligerent or menacing as it firmly insisted that each portion of its boundary line must be renegotiated and in some spots drawn anew. While recognizing that until this was accomplished the problem could not be satisfactorily resolved, the Chinese also let it be known that they were nonetheless prepared to live with the existing regime on their borders for the moment and to bide their time. Its claim properly staked out, Peking could afford to sit back and wait for the other party to tire of the game and head for the bargaining table or, if worst came to worst, put a modicum of pressure in the right place to hasten the conference or, in extremis, heat up the local temperature slightly to convince the opposite camp of the wisdom of attempting to settle the affair in friendly fashion without further delay. None of this impresses the objective onlooker as intrinsically unreasonable, nor will the recorded practice sustain any of the gory tales since circulated which strain to discredit the leaders of the PRC by trying to cast them in the role of megalomaniacs bent on conquering half the world in pursuit of a dream to restore the Middle Kingdom as it stood when at the pinnacle of its power and splendor.[54]

No doubt the flare-up on the Sino-Indian border for a while succeeded in injecting a jarring note into this tableau of serenity and self-restraint; it did not, however, seriously impugn the regional image Peking was striving to project, since in the surrounding countries—and, indeed, elsewhere as well—the uneasy feeling often prevailed that the Indians through their own stubbornness had contributed mightily to sparking the eruption and that the Chinese had demonstrated superior tactical skill by winning on the battlefield and then unilaterally withdrawing from the areas they had overrun. Having thus vindicated the status quo by force of arms, they left the other side with no option but to maintain the de facto boundary line or assume the responsibility for trying to alter it by military means, thereby placing India in a very awkward position in the eyes of the international community.

NOTES

    1. Text in The Important Documents of the First Plenary Session of the Chinese PPCC, Peking, 1949, and A. P. Blaustein (ed.), Fundamental Legal Documents of Communist China, South Hackensack, N.J.: Rothman and Co., 1962, pp. 34-53; text in Russian in E. F. Kovalev (ed.), Zakonodatelnye akty Kitaiskoi Narodnoi Respubliki, Moscow, 1952, pp. 50-65, and Obrazovanie Kitaiskoi Narodnoi Respubliki, dokumenty i materialy, Moscow, 1950, pp. 30-49.

    2. For a current elaboration of this theme by Soviet writers, see, for instance, E.A. Grigor'eva, E.D. Kostikov, "Spekulyatsiya maoistov ponyatiem 'neravnopravnyi dogovor'," Problemy Dalnego Vostoka, 1975, No. 1, pp. 54-55.

    3. Sbornik deistvuyushchikh dogovorov, soglashenii i konventsii, zaklyuchennykh SSSR s inostrannymi gosudarstvami, Moscow, 1925, Vol. 2, pp. 16-23 (hereafter, SDD); League of Nations Treaty Series, Vol. 37, pp. 175-91; L. Shapiro (ed.), Soviet Treaty Series, Washington, D.C.: Georgetown University Press, 1950, Vol. 1, pp. 242-43.

    4. An interesting technical argument has developed around the use of the term "redemarcation" in the various texts of the 1924 agreement. According to E. A. Grigor'eva, E. D. Kostikov, op. cit., pp. 57-58, here is what is involved. The 1924 Sino-Soviet agreement was signed in an English-language version only, whereas the Chinese and Russian language texts are just official translations. Article 7 of the English edition of the agreement stated that "the Governments of the two Contracting Parties agree to redemarcate their national boundaries. . . ." The Russian translation, instead of using the word "redemarkirovat" (to redemarcate) which then was not yet commonly accepted, used the expression "vnov proverit" which can literally be rendered as "verify anew" or "recheck." The Chinese- and English-language editions of the PRC government statement of May 24, 1969, in which reference was made to this provision of the 1924 agreement, correctly employed the word "redemarcate" and its proper Chinese equivalent. In the Russian-language edition of the statement, however, the Chinese not only did not use the now standard term "redemarkirovat," but even did not reproduce the term used in the official Russian translation of the agreement, that is, "verify anew" or "recheck." Instead, they offered their own translation of "vnov opredelit" which means to

"determine anew," synonymous, according to the Russian commentators, to "redelimit." The latter expression has, of course, a much broader connotation than "redemarcate." By this sleight-of-hand, the Russians claim, the Chinese tried to create the impression that the 1924 agreement sanctioned a "redrawing" of the boundary line and escalate a simple technical problem, "perhaps pregnant with conflict situations, but not going beyond the framework of ordinary questions of border relations," into a major political issue.

5. "Statement of the Government of the People's Republic of China, May 24, 1969," Peking Review, 1969, No. 22, p. 6 (hereafter, PR); China Reconstructs, 1969, No. 7, Suppl., p. 4 (hereafter, CR).

According to M. S. Kapitsa, Sovetsko-Kitaiskie otnosheniya, Moscow, 1958, pp. 154-55, citing Soviet archives, the conference opened in August 1925. The subcommissions which it created sat more or less regularly until April 1926. The text of a consular convention was drafted. The only item left unresolved was the Soviet proposal that the consuls have the right concurrently to function as personnel of the People's Commissariat for Foreign Trade, the right to include in the staff of the consulate the necessary number of employees, and the right to dispatch diplomatic couriers. A Chinese draft of a trade treaty was discussed, but since it did not take into account the Soviet Union's monopoly of foreign trade it proved unacceptable to the Russians, whereas the Soviet draft submitted at the end of 1925 was rejected by the Chinese. Beginning in March 1926, the subcommissions dealing with the trade treaty and the consular convention no longer met due to the illness of the Chinese representative. The legal subcommission drafted a convention on the extradition of criminals and a treaty on legal assistance in civil matters. A convention on inheritance also raised no difficulties. The subcommission on the demarcation of the frontier only held three meetings. The subcommission on claims was presented a Chinese claim in the amount of forty million gold rubles, primarily in compensation for material losses suffered by Chinese traders in connection with the revolution in Russia and the devaluation of the ruble.

In an interesting attempt to discredit the Communist Chinese leadership by bracketing it with the policies of its "reactionary" predecessors, F. Nikolayev, "How Peking Falsifies History," International Affairs, 1973, No. 5, p. 28, notes that "in 1925-1926 the militarist clique in power in Peking put forward far-reaching demands for a revision of the Soviet frontier in favor of China. Since then Chinese nationalists of all shades have been claiming primordial Soviet territories, including the Maritime region and the territory along the Amur."

6. Pravda, Aug. 27, 1945, and Izvestiya, Aug. 28, 1945; Vedomosti Verkhovnogo Soveta SSSR, 1945, No. 59; United Nations Treaty Series, 1947, Vol. 10, pp. 314-15, 322-23, 342-44.

7. A. Kruchinin, V. Olgin, Territorial Claims of Mao Tse-tung: History and Modern Times, Moscow, n.d., p. 25. Likewise, V. S. Myasnikov, A. G. Yakovlev, in Kitai segodnya, Moscow, 1969, p. 258, who add that: "For territorial claims to the MPR there were no real grounds, and their very enunciation ran counter to the then current course of the PRC's foreign policy; however, in Peking the raising of the question of the MPR was seen as an exploratory step: what if something should come of it! Nevertheless, Mao's main goal was to secure the political and economic support of the USSR. Having received this support, he shelved the question of collecting the lands of the Chinese empire until other, more propitious times."

8. Vedomosti Verkhovnogo Soveta SSSR, 1950, No. 36; SDD, Moscow, 1957, Vol. 14, pp. 17-19; UNTS, 1956, Vol. 226, pp. 10-11, 16-19.

9. This may explain the otherwise anomalous passage encountered in Vice-Premier Ch'en Yi's remarks at a press conference summoned on September 29, 1965, and attended by Chinese and foreign newsmen. Recalling that "in 1945 Chiang Kai-shek's government concluded a treaty with the Government of the Soviet Union recognizing the Mongolian People's Republic," he observed that "after its founding, New China succeeded to the commitment and recognized Mongolia as a socialist country" (emphasis added). Vice-Premier Ch'en Yi Answers Questions Put by Correspondents, Peking, 1966, p. 21.

Two further observations are in order here. First, the remark may have been somewhat less innocuous in intent than it sounds, for the speaker could thus have also been making the subtle point that the responsibility for acceding to Mongolia's independence lay with the Kuomintang (KMT) regime, that the PRC was then confronted with a fait accompli which was not of its own doing and that it would not have gone along with such a scheme if it had had to make the initial decision and was only willing to do so now because it was a matter of "succeeding to the [earlier] commitment." Second, even so, Ch'en Yi's wording was not quite accurate. The PRC did not automatically succeed, in the classical sense, to the legitimate commitments of its predecessor; the obligation did not routinely devolve from the KMT to the PRC and the latter did not act as though it were duty-bound to "inherit" the existing arrangement, but chose to give its positive consent to preserving the legal continuity, which presumably it had the option (at least in principle) of withholding.

10. Quoted by Hungdah Chiu, "Certain Legal Aspects of Communist China's Treaty Practice," ASIL Proceedings, 1967, p. 124.

11. Ibid.

12. Cf., Neville Maxwell, "Simmering Dispute along the Sino-Soviet Border," Times (London), Sept. 30, 1968, p. 9: "That is the

approach China has taken to the question of boundary settlement with all her neighbors. She has insisted in every case that the boundaries should be negotiated anew. But while refusing to accept the legality of boundaries imposed by the imperialists, she has in every case shown herself willing to accept the general alignments drawn by those imperialists. Such was the case in China's boundary settlements with Burma, Pakistan, and Afghanistan; and in her settlements with Mongolia and Nepal, China agreed to the boundaries that those smaller neighbors claimed. All these governments found that her interest was not in regaining territory but in removing what the Chinese saw as the stains of history. They found China tough but reasonable at the negotiating table and they emerged with their boundaries confirmed on the alignments they claimed, with minor variations upon which they had agreed with the Chinese in a pragmatic process of give and take."

13. Except, of course, that a proximate physical demarcation of the boundary line between the two countries was urgently needed since only short sections of it were ever surveyed and properly defined and riverine boundaries, especially on major navigational waterways and in fluvial basins which provide much of the livelihood for a relatively dense population on both banks of the stream, are notoriously productive of disputes and require complex, up-to-date treaties to sanction them. As a matter of practical importance, then, an on-the-spot delimitation of their joint frontier was long overdue.

14. Izvestiya, Feb. 15, 1950; SDD, Vol. 14, pp. 15-17; UNTS, Vol. 226, pp. 5-9, 12-17.

15. For example, Soviet government statement of March 29, 1969, Soviet News, 1969, No. 5483, p. 4, and excerpts in New York Times, Mar. 31, 1961, p. 16; A. Kruchinin, V. Olgin, op. cit., p. 28; O. B. Borisov, B. T. Koloskov, Sovetsko-Kitaiskie otnosheniya 1945-1970, kratkii ocherk, Moscow, 1971, pp. 271, 441; A. Denisov, "Geograficheskie 'izyskaniya' Pekina," Novoe vremya, 1972, No. 33, p. 15; V. S. Olgin, "Ekspansionizm v pogranichnoi politike Pekina," Problemy Dalnego Vostoka, 1975, No. 1, p. 45; V. S. Myasnikov, A. G. Yakovlev, op. cit., p. 274.

The evidence of the Statement of the PRC government of May 24, 1969, CR, 1969, No. 7, Suppl., p. 4, to the effect that the Sino-Soviet treaty of friendship, alliance, and mutual assistance is "in no sense a treaty or agreement for the settlement of the boundary question" and that still less can it "prove that there does not exist a boundary question between China and the Soviet Union" is inconclusive on that score. Technically speaking, the Chinese are right in that, whatever its significance for the broader territorial issue, the accord could not have been intended to determine a specific alignment of the boundary line or freeze the status quo as regards the concrete location of the frontier.

16. Sekai shūhō, Tokyo, Aug. 11, 1964; Pravda, Sept. 2, 1964; Current Digest of the Soviet Press, 1964, No. 34, pp. 6-7. The July 11, 1964, issue of the People's Daily (Peking) merely reported that on the previous day (July 10) Chairman Mao received thirty Japanese friends and had a "personal and friendly talk with them." No mention was made of the contents of the conversation, however.

17. Pravda, Sept. 2, 1964; In Connection with Mao Tse-tung's Talk with a Group of Japanese Socialists, Moscow, 1964, pp. 11-12; International Affairs, 1964, No. 10, p. 83; Current Digest of the Soviet Press, 1964, No. 34, p. 5.

Cf., B. Zanegin, Nationalist Background of China's Foreign Policy, Moscow, n.d., p. 47: "It follows that Peking permits the preservation of colonies on Chinese territory and at the same time attempts to deprive a socialist nation of its sovereignty." Also, A. Kruchinin, V. Olgin, op. cit., p. 25: "It was pointed out to him [Mao Tse-tung] in this connection that the issue could be settled only by the Mongolian people themselves as only they have the right to decide the fate of their own statehood. But this was a language Mao could not understand, for his chauvinistic mentality was incapable of accepting that a relatively small nation could claim the right to decide its own destiny. In his view the destinies of small nations should be resolved on the basis of 'the right of force'."

18. E. D. Kostikov, "Velikoderzhavnye ambitsii i pogranichnaya politika pekinskogo rukovodstva," Problemy Dalnego Vostoka, 1973, No. 1, p. 59.

19. Edgar Snow, Red Star Over China, rev. ed., New York: Random House, 1938, pp. 88-89, note 1. More recently, the exchange of letters between the PRC and the Soviet Union of February 14, 1950, which confirmed Mongolia's right to self-rule used, interestingly enough, the expression "independent status" (tu-li ti-wei in the Chinese original; nezavisimoe polozhenie in the Russian text) in describing Mongolia's current position, not plain "independence." This may be a normal circumlocution in the Chinese language, but sounds strange in Russian and English: "independent status" and "nezavisimoe polozhenie" intimate a temporal quality, a de facto phenomenon, with distinct undertones of impermanence. "Independence" conveys the flavor of something fixed, crystallized; "status" fluctuates. Another possible—and more innocuous—explanation for the choice of words might lie in the wish to avoid any suggestion that "independence" was not being granted by the PRC to Mongolia and, instead, to stress the point that the present correspondence merely aimed at confirming the existing "independent status" of Outer Mongolia stemming from the 1945 referendum and ratified by the establishment in the meantime of diplomatic relations between the two countries. Or, less innocently, the reason might lie in Peking's

desire to accentuate the fait accompli nature of the situation and imply that it was a mere victim of circumstances beyond its control (see note 9 above).

To compound the uncertainty, this particular diplomatic exchange (which the Chinese Communists formally designate as a joint "public statement") was not published in the PRC's official treaty series, although it did appear in the compilation Chung-hua jen-min kung-ho-kuo tui-wai kuan-hsi wen-chien chi 1949-1950, Peking, 1957, Vol. 1, pp. 74-75.

20. Izvestiya, Oct. 12, 1954; SDD, Vol. 16, pp. 12-24; People's China, Nov. 1, 1954, Suppl., pp. 4-5; UNTS, Vol. 226, pp. 56-57.

21. J. C. Hsiung, Law and Policy in China's Foreign Relations, A Study of Attitudes and Practice, New York and London: Columbia University Press, 1972, p. 57.

22. For example, O. B. Borisov, B. T. Koloskov, op. cit., p. 441; S. G. Yurkov, "50 let Sovetsko-Kitaiskikh otnoshenii," Problemy Dalnego Vostoka, 1974, No. 2, p. 69.

23. Asahi Shimbun, Tokyo, Aug. 1, 1964; D. J. Doolin, Territorial Claims in the Sino-Soviet Conflict, Stanford, Hoover Institution Studies No. 7, 1965, pp. 45-46.

24. Statement by the Government of the People's Republic of China on the Declaration of the Soviet Government on Relations Among Socialist States, Nov. 1, 1956, in P. E. Zinner (ed.), National Communism and Popular Revolt in Eastern Europe, New York: Columbia University Press, 1956, pp. 492-95.

25. Pravda, Oct. 31, 1956; Pod znamenem proletarskogo internatsionalizma, sbornik materialov, Moscow, 1957, pp. 15-18.

26. See note 24.

27. Izvestiya, Jan. 19, 1957; Deklaratsii, kayavleniya i kommyunike Sovetskogo pravitelstva s pravitelstvami inostrannykh gosudarstv 1954-1957 gg., Moscow, 1957, pp. 189-97.

28. For example, O. B. Borisov, B. T. Koloskov, op. cit., p. 441.

29. Statement of the Government of the People's Republic of China, May 24, 1969, PR, 1969, No. 22, p. 8, and CR, 1969, No. 7, Suppl., p. 6; Declaration of the Government of the USSR of Mar. 29, 1969, Pravda, Mar. 30, 1961; Izvestiya, Mar. 30, 1969; Soviet News, 1969, No. 5483, pp. 3-4, 14. See, too, A. Kruchinin, V. Olgin, op. cit., p. 32.

30. Statement of the PRC Government, May 24, 1969, PR, 1969, No. 22, p. 7; CR, 1969, No. 7, Suppl., p. 5.

31. O. B. Borisov, B. T. Koloskov, op. cit., pp. 303-4.

32. Ibid., p. 272; O. Borisov, B. Koloskov, "Politika Sovetskogo Soyuza v otnoshenii KNR—sotsialisticheskii internatsionalism v

deistvii (sovetsko-kitaiskie otnosheniya v 1948-1967gg.),'' in Leninskaya politika SSSR v otnoshenii Kitaya, Moscow, 1968, p. 186; M. S. Kapitsa, Eskalatsiya verolomstva (Politika Pekina i Sovetsko-Kitaiskie otnosheniya), Moscow, 1970, pp. 11-12; A. Kruchinin, V. Olgin, op. cit., p. 92.

33. A. Kruchinin, V. Olgin, op. cit., p. 93.

34. M. S. Kapitsa, Levee zdravogo smysla (O vneshnei politike gruppy Mao), Moscow, 1968, pp. 67-68; idem, KNR: dva desyatiletiya-dve politiki, Moscow, 1969, p. 194; S. G. Yurkov, Pekin: novaya politika?, Moscow, 1972, p. 59.

35. A. Kruchinin, V. Olgin, op. cit., p. 92.

36. O. B. Borisov, B. T. Koloskov, op. cit., p. 272. The authors add that "only thanks to the restraint of the Soviet frontier guards was it possible to prevent their escalation to major incidents." Even so, according to M. S. Kapitsa, KNR, p. 194, it was only in June 1962 that "there began systematic provocations on the frontier with the USSR"; hence, what happened before that must have been rather minor.

37. O. B. Borisov, B. T. Koloskov, op. cit., pp. 271, 441; M. S. Kapitsa, op. cit. (note 32 above), p. 11; O. Ivanov, "Soviet-Chinese Relations: Truth and Fiction," Socialism: Theory and Practice, 1975, No. 1, Suppl., p. 52 (originally published in Mirovaya ekonomika i mezhdunarodnye otnosheniya, 1974, No. 8).

38. USSR Government Statement of Mar. 29, 1969, Pravda, Mar. 30, 1969.

39. PR, 1969, No. 22, p. 8; CR, 1969, No. 7, Suppl., p. 6.

40. The latest such incident involves the publication in Peking in 1972 of a World Atlas containing maps (especially Nos. 4 and 38) to which strong objections have been raised in Soviet literature. See, for example, A. Denisov, loc. cit.; G. Apalin, "Geografiya po-maoistski," Izvestiya, Aug. 7, 1972; E. D. Kostikov, op. cit., p. 62.

41. Liu Pei-hua (ed.), Chung-kuo chin-tai chien-shih, Peking, 1954, following p. 253. Reproduced in D. J. Doolin, op. cit., p. 16, and New York Times, Sept. 6, 1964, part 4, p. 3.

42. The Nepalese government apparently learned of the chart and its reference to Nepal during a visit of the Nepalese Prime Minister to the PRC, where Nepalese students in Peking brought it to his attention. Mongolia, as might have been expected, followed the Soviet lead and began denouncing Chinese cartographic practice vis-a-vis the MPR at the same time as the Russians started criticizing Chinese map treatment of the USSR-PRC frontier. Thus, "Falshivye karty, Rasskaz mongolskogo studenta, obuchavshegosya v Pekine," Pravda, July 30, 1964.

43. On a more modest scale, the same can be said of the

Chinese. Indeed, according to the Statement of the Soviet Government of Mar. 29, 1969: "At the request of the Chinese side, the Soviet Union delivered to the PRC at the beginning of the 1950s complete sets of topographical maps showing the line of the frontier. The Chinese authorities made no comment at the time on the position of the frontier line shown on the maps, and that line was observed in practice." Pravda, Mar. 30, 1961. See. too, O. B. Borisov, B. T. Koloskov, op. cit., pp. 271. 441.

Attempts by the Russians to translate this silence into prima facie evidence of positive acquiescence by the PRC in the version of the boundary line featured in these Soviet cartographic surveys has, technically speaking, little persuasive value, for the Chinese were under no legal duty to respond (protest) stricto sensu and thus did not forfeit any rights by exercising their privilege to keep quiet. Besides, the argument cuts both ways: if Chinese failure to file a formal complaint here can be construed as an expression of tacit "recognition," a fortiori, certainly the same conclusion applies to the more glaring absence of any official Soviet reaction to far stronger and more frequent "provocations" of this type.

44. "Quarterly Chronicle and Documentation," China Quarterly, 1964, No. 18, p. 241.

45. For various elaborations of these themes, see E. D. Kostikov, op. cit., pp. 57-62; V. S. Olgin, "Ekspansionizm v pogranichnoi politike Pekina," Problemy Dalnego Vostoka, 1975, No. 1, p. 39; A. Kruchinin, V. Olgin, op. cit., pp. 13, 29-32.

Soviet authors make much of the fact that the reported armed clashes on the PRC's frontiers with several of the neighboring states have occurred in the areas marked on Chinese maps as "lost" or where the frontier was described as "undetermined." The examples they cite include Burma in 1955, India in 1959 and 1962, Nepal in 1960, and the Soviet Union in 1969 (see, E. D. Kostikov, op. cit., p. 59). What Soviet commentators fail to mention and perhaps to realize in this connection is: 1) that all the instances referred to concern countries with whom the PRC at that time did not have its own boundary treaty or, for that matter, still does not; and, 2) if border clashes were to occur, they would, quite logically, tend to happen where the boundary line was already in dispute. Thus, the Soviet argument that "cartographic aggression" or "cartographic war" was the deliberate precursor to a "shooting affray" could easily be turned around into the proposition that the occurrence of the clashes at precisely these locations objectively proves that they were trouble spots that urgently needed taking care of by appropriate diplomatic means. While Soviet spokesmen do not mention the possibility of a "natural coincidence" between the two factors, the mere availability of an alternative explanation for this phenomenon does not, of course, automatically vitiate the Soviet contention that the PRC could have been actively staging border conflicts at particular junctures of the frontier either to dramatize its grandiose territorial claims or "to blackmail" the other side into entering into negotiations on a "comprehensive boundary settlement" in accordance with the PRC's pet modus operandi.

46. E. D. Kostikov, op. cit., p. 58.

47. Soviet authors, however, claim differently. For instance, according to E. D. Kostikov, "Politicheskaya kartografiya na sluzhbe velikoderzhavnogo natsionalizma," Problemy Dalnego Vostoka, 1973 No. 4, p. 90, the publication of such maps was designed to educate the popular masses in a nationalist and chauvinist spirit and their insertion in school books shows that the group of Mao Tse-tung pursued from the outset the aim of brainwashing China's youth in the spirit of "Great Han nationalism." No solid evidence is offered in support of this assertion and the mere inclusion of these maps in instructional materials is treated as sufficient to warrant the above assertion. To others, the connection may not seem either obvious or unassailable.

The only other evidence adduced by the Russians to substantiate the charge that the Mao regime sought "to place territorial questions in the public eye" and "fan chauvinistic sentiments among the people" involves "a broad discussion" conducted in 1961-62 in the Chinese press on the limits of China's state territory in various historical epochs. In the process, the Manchu dynasty and Genghis Khan were reportedly glorified because of their association with huge empires and periods of territorial aggrandizement (A. Kruchinin, V. Olgin, op. cit., pp. 32-33; O. B. Borisov, B. T. Koloskov, op. cit., pp. 273-74). Such a one-shot operation, focusing, in addition, on rather esoteric historical themes, would hardly appear to qualify for the kind of sustained "propaganda workout" that would be required to transform the frontier question into a passionate national issue. References to learned articles in scientific journals, couched along similar lines and published in 1964, prove the point even less.

48. Li Tsung-jen and Chang Hsin-hai, Letter to the Editor, New York Times, Sept. 18, 1963, p. 38.

49. Peter S. H. Tang, Russian Expansion into the Maritime Province: The Contemporary Soviet and Chinese Communist Views, Washington, D. C.: Research Institute on the Sino-Soviet Bloc, 1962, p. 47.

50. Ibid.

51. New York Times, Feb. 26, 1961, p. 20.

52. Quoted by F. Watson, The Frontiers of China, New York: Praeger, 1966, pp. 87-88.

53. See, for example, "Huang Chi-hsiang Unmasked as a Two-

faced, Anti-Communist, and Anti-Socialist Monster," New China News Agency (NCNA), Peking, July 29, 1957.

It is interesting to note that some Soviet authors take the Chinese leadership to task for not having moved fast enough to muzzle the criticism and for not having formally repudiated these "rightist slanders" against the Soviet Union at the time. They maintain that both the procrastination and the omission were deliberate, that this indicates that Mao secretly sympathized with the views thus expressed (although for current tactical reasons he eventually moved to suppress their public utterance), and that he consciously used the occasion surreptitiously to spread his own "doctrines." See, O. B. Borisov, B. T. Koloskov, op. cit., pp. 89, 272; A. Kruchinin, V. Olgin, op. cit., p. 31; Vneshnyaya politika i mezhdunarodnye otnosheniya Kitaiskoi Narodnoi Respubliki 1949-1973, Moscow, 1974, Vol. 1, pp. 53-54.

54. Cf., E. D. Kostikov, op. cit. (note 18 above), p. 56.

2

THE SOVIET OFFENSIVE

KHRUSHCHEV'S SPEECH TO THE
SUPREME SOVIET, 1962

The opening salvo in the war of words (before they turned into bullets on several occasions during 1969) was fired by the Soviet side. Stung to the quick by Peking's accusations of "adventurism" in first introducing missiles into Cuba and "capitulationism" in then removing them under U.S. pressure, Khrushchev, in his speech before the Supreme Soviet on December 12, 1962, launched a broad counterattack against his Chinese critics. Quoting the relevant passage in his address in full will serve to pinpoint the proper sequence of these events and permit a more precise analysis of the complexion of the ensuing altercation. Said Khrushchev to the detractors of his role during the Caribbean crisis:

> One must be very cautious and not rush in with irresponsible charges, such as that some carry out an orthodox policy while others pursue a mistaken policy, some are attacking imperialism and do not tolerate it, while others allegedly display liberalism. These questions can be rightly understood, and different actions can be correctly assessed, only if one takes into account the time, place, and circumstances in which one has to operate.
> India, for instance, achieved the liberation of Goa, Diu, and Daman. Those were vestiges of colonialism on Indian soil. Even when the British colonialists had been expelled from India, Portugal retained her colonies there, colonies which disseminated the foul stench of colonialism. India, and her government, showed patience and tolerated this for several years, but then threw out the colonialists. Did they act rightly? Of

course, they did! Incidentally, when this question was discussed in the Security Council, the United States and Great Britain tried, in point of actual fact, to have India proclaimed an aggressor. They tried to set the public opinion of the world against India. It was only the veto of the Soviet Union that prevented them from achieving this.

One more example. When Indonesia gained her freedom, the Dutch colonialists tried to retain West Irian. The Indonesian people and their government, however, compelled the colonialists to withdraw from West Irian.

We did what we could to help Indonesia in her struggle, and we welcome the liberation of West Irian, and her reunification with free Indonesia.

Macao is situated at the mouth of the Chuchiang River, on the coast of China. It is a small territory and not easily to be spotted on the map. It was leased by the Portuguese way back in the middle of the sixteenth century and in 1887 they wrested it completely from China and made it their colony. The British colony of Hong Kong is there also—it lies in the Delta of the Hsichiang River, literally below the heart of such an important town as Kwangchow (Canton). The odour coming from these places is by no means sweeter than that which was released by colonialism in Goa.

But no one will denounce the People's Republic of China for leaving these fragments of colonialism intact.

It would be wrong to prod China into actions of some kind which she considers untimely. If the government of the People's Republic of China tolerates Macao and Hong Kong it clearly has good reason for doing so. It would, therefore, be ridiculous to levy against it the accusation that these are concessions to the British and Portuguese colonialists, that this is appeasement.

But perhaps that is a retreat from Marxism-Leninism? Nothing of the kind! It means that the government of the People's Republic of China is taking into account reality, the acutal possibilities.

And this is by no means because the Chinese are less sensitive to colonialism than the Indians, that they are more tolerant towards Salazar than India is. No, our Chinese friends hate colonialism just as every revolutionary does. But they are clearly basing themselves on their conditions, they are acting in accordance with their own views and are showing patience.

But does this mean that we must condemn them for this, that we must claim that they have retreated from

Marxism-Leninism? No, it doesn't. That would be ridiculous.

As a result of a variety of conditions, one sometimes has to live not among fragrant roses but amidst thorns and sometimes even in close proximity to the colonialists' outhouses.

But the hour will come when our Chinese friends will find this position intolerable and will tell the colonialists in a loud voice "Get out!" And we shall welcome that step. But it is for our Chinese friends themselves to decide when this is to be done.

We are not hurrying them. On the contrary, we say: "Decide this matter in the way that your country's interests, and the interests of the whole socialist camp, demand."[1]

The thrust of the Soviet leader's argument thus lay in a plea for a pragmatic approach to vital questions of foreign affairs, eschewing dogmatic judgments and rigid doctrinal slogans in favor of effective tactics and practical considerations. He did more, though, than simply call for a halt to ideological recriminations between the PRC and the Soviet Union, for he went beyond the mere passive defense of the merits of his administration's past performance in the field of international politics and, in turn, proceeded to find fault with various aspects of the Communist Chinese diplomatic record to date. The important dimension here is the stylistic element which offers the best clue to Khrushchev's motivations in choosing to answer his opponents and his probable intentions in broaching this particular line of inquiry.

A direct confrontation on the main issues was studiously avoided. To be sure, the juxtaposition of Peking's seeming indifference to the persistence of residues of colonialism on PRC territory and India's and Indonesia's evident determination to wipe out all traces of imperial rule from their soil was hardly flattering to the Chinese ego, especially at a juncture when relations between the PRC and India were thoroughly spoiled. The invidious comparison was meant to embarrass the PRC advocates of "revolutionary purism" —and the gambit obviously succeeded. At the same time, Khrushchev was very careful to protect his own flanks. While lauding the Indians and Indonesians for their dispatch in sweeping away the remnants of colonial domination from their shores and publicly reaffirming the Soviet Union's support for anyone who acted likewise, the Soviet chief insisted that he was not lecturing his Chinese allies on how to manage their private business. Nevertheless, the implication was clear enough—in his estimate, the non-Communist Indians and Indonesians had so far proved more hostile to surviving manifestations of colonialism in their backyard than had the Chinese comrades despite their oft-avowed hatred for all things imperialist.

True, the Soviet premier professed mild surprise at how accommodating the PRC government's attitude toward its sworn enemies looked to him, but again hastened to emphasize that he had no desire to advise the PRC leadership on the manner of dealing with the existing anomalous situation and no wish to egg it on into initiating rash measures to eject the British and Portuguese from their footholds in Hong Kong and Macao. Indeed, the closing reference to "the interests of the whole socialist camp" tempered somewhat the previous impression the Soviet head of state had created, inadvertently perhaps, that he was giving his Chinese associates completely free rein in disposing of this problem.

Weighed in substantive terms, Khrushchev's message sounded quite innocuous. What he said was not new; what was significant was how he said it. Reiterating the Soviet Union's unqualified endorsement of the "struggle by the emergent nations to eliminate all local vestiges of the colonial heritage" could not per se be expected to upset the Chinese, although singling out India and Indonesia for elaborate praise in this context was certain to irk the PRC hierarchy because of its running feud with these countries. Expressing the hope that Communist China too would some day soon expel the colonialists from Hong Kong and Macao was not, on the face of it, an offensive comment either, even if the accompanying allusion to the PRC's marked slowness in tackling the job was bound to grate on Peking's nerves. Plainly, Khrushchev was throwing a few digs at his Chinese "friends." Yet, the needling was sufficiently subtle that the victim was denied a solid excuse to take umbrage; the wording was unobjectionable, the tone and accent had a cutting edge to them, hence, in the final analysis, it all boiled down to personal interpretation, leaving the responsibility for the next move up to those at whom the remarks were aimed and, in fact, inviting the latter to show their hand by bidding or dropping out of the game while also deftly shifting onto their shoulders the onus for any ensuing "escalation" of the polemic. Meantime, Khrushchev could easily plead innocence should the Chinese claim they felt affronted by his language; and should they lash back at him he could just as readily protest that his statement had been misunderstood or deliberately distorted by the leaders of the PRC bent on picking a quarrel.

In a technical sense, one further item bears noting, since it reflected an effort by Khrushchev to establish a definite limit to the discussion he was prepared to engage in by drawing a firm distinction between the kinds of territorial problems he had in mind when urging the systematic expulsion of colonial powers from their sundry overseas possessions. He left no doubt that he was talking about conflicts that pitted imperial states endeavoring to keep their dominions against nations from whose land these had originally been carved out. Frontier disputes between two recognized and independent countries fell into an altogether separate category (and, of course, nothing in Khrushchev's words contained the slightest hint that similar difficulties could ever arise between "socialist" states).

THE SOVIET REACTION TO THE CHINESE-INDIAN DISPUTE

Commenting on the recent large-scale fighting between the PRC and India, Khrushchev unequivocally deplored such use of force and the attendant heavy casualties each belligerent suffered. "This has grieved us deeply," he said. "On the question of border disputes we maintain Leninist views," he claimed and proceeded to explain that "the forty-five-year experience of the Soviet Union suggests that there are no border disputes which, provided there is a mutual desire to do so, cannot be settled without resort to arms. It is from these positions that Soviet people approach the developments on the Chinese-Indian border."[2] All subsequent Soviet pronouncements on the subject have echoed these parallel themes that no boundary disagreement warrants use of force to impose a solution and that, given a modicum of good will, an acceptable answer can always be worked out through diplomatic media.

Both sides were accordingly blamed in this instance for allowing the argument to degenerate into violence and exhorted to compose their differences amicably, with greater accent, however, on Peking's role in first starting the brawl and later unilaterally suspending hostilities by pulling its troops back to the line they manned before their incursion into India's northern regions. Even so, the Chinese were simultaneously faulted for permitting the situation to get out of hand and praised for demonstrating restraint, "reasonableness," and "wisdom" in promptly terminating the unfortunate affair.[3] In sum, for the Soviets the entire incident was cause for deep regret, and they afforded their Chinese allies no material or spiritual aid or comfort in the military confrontation with India. Liquidating colonial regimes was apparently one thing, and to be warmly greeted; handling a border dispute between "friendly states" through recourse to armed might was taboo. Moscow hoped to be able to convince Peking not to confuse the two.

KHRUSHCHEV'S TACTICS: TWO HYPOTHESES

With all due respect for Khrushchev's skill in framing these issues in a manner best calculated to avoid a direct clash with his Communist Chinese confederates—counting on ambiguous formulas and casuistic qualifications to slant the dialogue in his favor or, alternatively, to furnish him with a convenient escape-route—one nonetheless wonders at what could have motivated him to inject so dangerous a topic as the territorial issue into the ongoing debate with the Chinese critics of his administration's foreign and domestic policy. Notwithstanding the multiple semantic precautions he took, springing the territorial question itself in the light of the documented record of past Russo-Chinese history seems a rather fool-hardy gesture by most standards. A couple of hypotheses may account for the choice of tactics.

To begin with, the leaders of the PRC had previously made several determined attempts to involve their Soviet counterparts in a substantive discussion of the profile of the existing frontiers of the Soviet Union. Soviet officials must have found these recurrent surreptitious efforts to extract what to them looked like consequential territorial concessions from the Soviet Union extremely annoying and possibly Khrushchev finally decided that, under the circumstances, he had nothing to lose and even stood to gain a bit by trying to smoke the Chinese out into the open on this particular item. Since the PRC spokesmen persisted in wanting to deal with this matter in private conversations, perhaps Khrushchev thought he might as well test their true intentions and either give them a chance to air their views properly or to stop striving to corral the Soviets into debating the proposition. In either case, he ran little risk and, indeed, was sure of posting a propaganda victory over his opponents: if the Chinese rose to the bait, they could then be widely exposed as "territorial revisionists," a potentially serious charge in the overheated atmosphere of Third World politics; if they declined, the Soviet head of state would have the satisfaction of having administered a stinging rebuff to Mao and his associates and forced them to beat a retreat on an important point.

Actually, this scenario has since gained added weight as information continues to trickle out on how common and frequent instances of palpable friction on the Sino-Soviet frontier had become on the eve of Khrushchev's "outburst." What at the time was perceived as a display of irritation and maybe even as an act of gross overreaction to Chinese "heckling" looks, in retrospect, very much like a fit of exasperation (a sentiment shared by both sides, perhaps). The full array of pressures exerted in this sector is still not known, but compared to the few trifling episodes hitherto either recorded or suspected, the evidence has mounted steadily that the accumulated experience of constant aggravations in this domain was gradually building up a residue of tension that could not be entirely dispelled by occasional moments of tranquillity in the frontier zone.

The PRC's diplomatic initiatives to broach the border issue started earlier and occurred more often than any outside observer of the scene might have expected. In 1960, the Buz-Aigyr incident had further complicated the situation and, according to new Soviet disclosures, in 1961-62 several thousand infringements of the boundary line by the Chinese were catalogued. Nor is the picture complete and once in a while Chinese sources, too, offer fresh glimpses of how ulcerous conditions here had grown as when in the sixties the Hong Kong Hsing Tao Daily featured a report about an island, wrongly identified as Chenpao Island, which Soviet troops had "occupied" back in the spring of 1959. Liu Shao-ch'i supposedly raised the issue of this island in the context of general border problems in the region during his 1960 visit to Moscow with no tangible results, for, after 1959, fifteen more intrusions were registered in the same spot which allegedly prompted three official protests by the Chinese government. How many more such controversies punctuated this period can only be guessed at, but odds are this is just a small sample of the lot.

In many ways, then, the real surprise is that it took so long for the pot to boil over considering the circumstances. Two factors may explain the singular lapse. First, the extreme doctrinal sensitivity of the whole business of territorial and/or border disputes within the precinct of the "socialist" community elicited an intense reluctance on the part of all concerned to tread on this dangerous ground, born of a priori conviction of the objective impropriety of that phenomenon under the norms of "intra-socialist" relations. Nor is there any reason to believe that the topic was not in fact treated with the utmost ideological gravity, as the forceful tone of the following pronouncement would tend to indicate:

> The attitude of proletarian political parties to national territorial problems, in particular, is a sure indicator of their international position, their loyalty to the struggle for socialism and the liberation of humanity from all forms of exploitation. It is the attitude to these problems in the history of the world liberation movement that has time and again revealed that "genuine revolutionaries," "the most loyal fighters" for the liberation of mankind, may turn out to be national chauvinists. . . .
> The great international struggle of the working class is never hampered more than by the influence of

nationalistic ideology. It is not by accident that Lenin paid so much attention to the national question, striving to the end to stamp out nationalistic prejudice in the international revolutionary workers' movement. He repeatedly stressed the need for consistent democracy in resolving the national question, regarding the right of nations to self-determination as a major basis for the elimination of obstacles to the closest class unity of the proletariat in all countries including all variations of chauvinistic views on questions of state territory. . . .

Socialist revolutions in principle eliminate territorial questions from relations between socialist states if the communist parties which head them conduct an internationalist policy, not in word, but in deed, and adhere in practice to the Marxist-Leninist principle of national self-determination.[4]

In light of these postulates, a profound aversion for being publicly tagged with the responsibility for triggering an argument over territorial issues vis-a-vis a fellow "socialist" state is quite understandable. Matters of dogma apart, however, calculations of expediency also entered the equation and played a key role in causing the Kremlin's stong allergy to inquiring into purported territorial or frontier disparities between the Soviet Union and another socialist state. The majority of the Soviet Union's continental neighbors today qualify as "socialist" states, most of them lost territory to the Soviet Union in times past, and any overt suggestion that territorial readjustments might be a legitimate topic of discussion within the "socialist" fraternity (say, versus the PRC) could encourage the rest of the members of the group with similar potential claims against the Soviet Union to agitate for a review of the status quo in their favor as well.

Such a prospect was hardly likely to appeal to the Soviet leadership and would probably induce it to avoid the subject almost at all cost. That Khrushchev finally succumbed to the temptation to try to pin his Chinese opponents on the cross of Hong Kong and Macao and thus risk injecting the territorial theme into the Sino-Soviet shouting match bespeaks the depth of his frustration with the Chinese comrades and their constant sniping at every aspect of his political performance. Note, though, that even at this crucial juncture, Khrushchev still kept sufficient control over his temper to discourse solely about the fate of various colonial possessions and never once mention the difficulties which the Soviet Union was experiencing with the PRC along their common boundary line. Yet, it is easy to imagine how he must have resented the spectacle of

the PRC's complacency toward the "imperialists" ensconced in
Hong Kong and Macao considering the troubles the Chinese were
simultaneously inflicting on their "socialist" brethren to the north.

The second theory hinges on a certain amount of available
evidence to the effect that at this point Khrushchev was under substantial pressure at home from the Stalinist or Maoist wing of the
Party and that the "territorial gambit" may have been conceived as
a deliberate ploy to outmaneuver his internal enemies: if he could
unmask the Chinese hierarchy by showing that it coveted Soviet soil,
the pro-Peking faction in the Kremlin would pro tanto be put on the
defensive by virtue of being labeled as ideologically aligned with a
regime purportedly bent on tearing vast stretches of land away from
Mother Russia. Even is the Chinese refused to take the bait, Khrushchev could still come out ahead: a major setback to the Chinese
"leftists" was bound to affect negatively the position of their local
adherents. Assuming the above interpretation to be correct, Khrushchev may here have turned one of the neatest tricks of his tortuous
career, since he obviously managed to weather the storm and survive a while longer.

On balance, it is hard to tell which of these results the Soviet
leader hoped for—a concrete Chinese reflex or a success by default.
With his temperament and from the perspective of the conditions in
which he had to operate, the prospect of publicly nailing his Chinese
adversaries probably attracted him more.

The preceding analysis calls for one last observation. The
critical ingredient in the foregoing picture lies in its proof of the
wholly contrived nature of the controversy's origins. There was no
concrete reason for Khrushchev to introduce the territorial issue
when he did. That step was dictated by ulterior motives of a purely
political order matched by reenforcing psychological impulses
(for example, anger, impatience) in no guise related to the drift
of the earlier comments by the Chinese authorities which presumably triggered the response. The roots of a phenomenon usually
determine its subsequent development, unless some new element
intervenes in midcourse and sends it off in a different direction.
Hence, the accidental provenance of the affair is vitally important
for the correct evaluation of the record since it serves to testify
to the inherent artificiality of the problem, if it cannot be shown that
an incremental factor has in the meantime entered the picture and
managed to alter the original formula: in this case, no trace can be
found of an additive capable of precipitating such a metamorphosis.
At any rate, nothing in the scenario of the episode's genesis conveyed
the sense of urgency or drama that generally surrounds the outbreak
of an earnest territorial dispute and in assessing the meaning of these
events that symptom must certainly be included in the end equation.

CHINESE REACTION

On January 9, 1963, the U.S. Communist party issued its own statement on "The Cuban Crisis and the Struggle for World Peace"[5] in which it repeated Khrushchev's references to Taiwan, Hong Kong, and Macao and lamented the PRC's embroilment in a military conflict with India "at the very moment when imperialism threatened the peace of the entire world." After a protracted silence, the Chinese side finally accepted the challenge and an editorial in People's Daily of March 8, 1963, took up the cudgels on Peking's behalf.[6] Noting that "some persons have mentioned Taiwan, Hong Kong, and Macao," the authors of the piece judged that "we are obliged to discuss a little of the history of imperialist aggression against China," which they did in the following terms:

> In the hundred years or so prior to the victory of the Chinese revolution, the imperialist and colonial powers—the United States, Britain, France, Tsarist Russia, Germany, Japan, Italy, Austria, Belgium, the Netherlands, Spain and Portugal—carried out unbridled aggression against China. They compelled the governments of old China to sign a large number of unequal treaties—the Treaty of Nanking of 1842, the Treaty of Aigun of 1858, the Treaty of Tientsin of 1858, the Treaty of Peking of 1860, the Treaty of Ili of 1881, the Protocol of Lisbon of 1887, the Treaty of Shimonoseki of 1895, the Convention for the Extension of Hongkong of 1898, the International Protocol of 1901, and so on. By virtue of these unequal treaties, they annexed Chinese territory in the north, south, east, and west and held leased territories on the seaboard and in the hinterland of China. Some seized Taiwan and the Penghu Islands, some occupied Hongkong and forcibly leased Kowloon, some put Macao under perpetual occupation, and so on.
>
> At the time the People's Republic of China was inaugurated, our government declared that it would examine the treaties concluded by previous Chinese governments with foreign governments, treaties that had been left by history, and would recognize, abrogate, revise or renegotiate them according to their respective contents. In this respect, our policy towards the socialist countries is fundamentally different from our policy towards the imperialist countries. When we deal with various imperialist countries, we take differing circumstances

into consideration and make distinctions in our policy. As a matter of fact, many of these treaties concluded in the past either have lost their validity, or have been abrogated, or have been replaced by new ones. With regard to the outstanding issues, which are a legacy from the past, we have always held that, when conditions are ripe, they should be settled peacefully through negotiations and that, pending a settlement, the <u>status quo</u> should be maintained. Within this category are the questions of Hongkong, Kowloon, and Macao and the questions of all those boundaries which have not been formally delimited by the parties concerned in each case. As for Taiwan and the Penghu Islands, they were restored to China in 1945, and the question now is the U.S. imperialist invasion and occupation of them and U.S. imperialist interference in China's internal affairs. We Chinese people are determined to liberate our own territory of Taiwan; at the same time, through the ambassadorial talks between China and the United States in Warsaw we are striving to solve the question of effecting the withdrawal of U. S. armed forces from Taiwan and the Taiwan Straits. Our position as described above accords not only with the interests of the Chinese people but also with the interests of the people of the socialist camp and the people of the whole world.

You are not unaware that such questions as those of Hongkong and Macao relate to the category of unequal treaties left over by history, treaties which the imperialists imposed on China. It may be asked: In raising questions of this kind, do you intend to raise all the questions of unequal treaties and have a general settlement? Has it ever entered your heads what the consequences would be? Can you seriously believe that this will do you any good?[7]

In short, if the Soviets were eager to talk about territorial problems, the Chinese were ready to accommodate them, but only on their own grounds, which happened not to coincide with those the Soviets had picked. Plainly, the tenor of the Chinese retort constituted in this respect a net aggravation of the quarrel between the two capitals.

For the first time, the validity of the mode of acquisition by Russia of certain areas once allegedly belonging to China was publicly contested by the PRC's official spokesmen. By branding, inter alia, the conventions of Aigun, Tientsin, Peking, and Ili—all of which consummated the transfer of chunks of Chinese soil to Russia—unequal treaties, the PRC leaders let it clearly be understood that, to their mind, these agreements as well as the cessions they ratified were in principle eo ipso illegal. Then, by quietly altering the wording of Article 55 of the Common Program and insinuating that by dint of this clause the new sovereign had expressly retained the right "to study treaties concluded by <u>previous Chinese governments</u> with foreign governments" (emphasis added), instead of, as in the authentic text, just those concluded by the Kuomintang, Peking effectively set the stage for the eventual recognition, abrogation, revision, or renegotiation of any of these pacts that such an examination might entail.

This is not to say, as has often been done, that the Communist Chinese were advancing claims for the immediate reversion to their jurisdiction of large tracts of land incorporated into the Soviet Union's Siberian provinces. To begin with, in adumbrating the subject of "unequal treaties," the writers of the essay were careful to couch their statements in highly tentative tones. Though the treaties in question were duly designated as unequal, Peking's advocates refrained from taking the next normal step of classifying them as automatically null and void. Rather, having made that crucial point, the Chinese switched around and rhetorically asked their allies whether they really wanted to pursue the topic further, in which case, presumably, the PRC authorities would be prepared to push the argument to its logical extreme. Otherwise, so ran the inference, they were quite disposed to call it quits on that note.

Nevertheless, one can hardly overestimate the potency of the psychological shock alone produced by this invocation of the "unequal treaties" alibi. Apparently, "true socialists" were simply not expected to talk to each other that way under any circumstances, no matter even if objective conditions might warrant the charge. By definition, the subject was off-limits for members of the "socialist" community in their intramural dealings, with no exceptions permitted to the rule. The Chinese had violated this peremptory injunction and thus had committed a cardinal sin. For, according to the Soviets:

> References by Chinese propaganda and Chinese diplomacy to the allegedly unequal character of the old treaties, helping to incite chauvinism in the Chinese people, instigate hatred for the Soviet Union and the fraternal Russian people, would be politically inadmissible even in the event they were historically accurate. Even in that event a genuine Communist ought not to stir up the past if that should serve not the strengthening of cooperation between

two great socialist powers, but the instigation of national hatred.[8]

Why bother to summon the controversial concept of "unequal treaties" at all, if it was not going to be used to its full extent? In part, one supposes, the act was intended to sound a serious warning for the future, should the Soviets persist in their present course: fresh carping by the Kremlin on the Maoist failure to vindicate the territorial integrity of China's home territory could impel the PRC government to press forthwith for the return of all ancestral lands, including those lost to Russia in the last century, with dire political consequences for the individuals rash enough to incur Peking's wrath. But, the PRC leadership may also have had an extra card hidden up its collective sleeve: if sufficiently rattled, perhaps the Soviets would blunder into rushing to the defense of the agreements, the legitimacy of which was being impugned, thereby enabling Peking to score a neat propaganda coup by baring to the eyes of the world the Khrushchev "clique's" true face as a self-confessed champion of international documents sanctioning the product of brutal colonial depredations. The risk of earning in the process the sobriquet of "territorial revisionist" would be more than balanced by the advantages accruing from publicly sticking Moscow with the tag of "territorial imperialist."

The scheme was surely worth testing. Either the Soviets would henceforward desist from trying to portray the Chinese as delinquent in protecting the country's physical heritage, or their borders with the PRC would become a live issue, forcing them somehow to prove bona fide title to much of their Far Eastern possessions—doctrinally not an easy project in view of the manner in which most of this property was originally obtained—or to fall back on quoting the provisions of the tsarist conventions—ideologically an altogether thankless task.

Meanwhile, the central thrust of Peking's message lay elsewhere. In practical terms, what the Chinese were telling the Soviets was that the frontier extant between the two states was in no sense final but awaited the same kind of exercise in joint redemarcation for which, according to Peking's version, the other sectors of the PRC's boundaries with neighboring nations had been slated from the very start. The facile illusion, hitherto widely shared, that the operative border-trace separating Soviet from Chinese territory was exempt from fresh scrutiny was thus rudely dispelled. The Soviets were by no means placed in an inferior position compared with the rest of the states that rubbed shoulders with the PRC. On the contrary, the Chinese took special pains to stress that, "in this respect, our policy towards the socialist countries is fundamentally different from our policy towards the imperialist countries," which at least implied that the path to diplomatic agreement would in this instance be smoother.

Still, the Chinese proposal manifestly envisaged businesslike bargaining sessions, a compromise settlement which would carry the signatures of the top leaders of the Soviet Union and the PRC in lieu of the names of representatives of the old order—in short, an official testimonial to the freely granted acquiescence of the PRC authorities in the contours of the ensuing Sino-Soviet frontier line rather than the previous odd situation where everyone simply assumed that the PRC's hands were tied by dusty relics of a distant past. As on earlier occasions, Peking accompanied its bid with standard assurances to the effect that it was in no hurry to tackle the job, that it wished for a peaceful answer to these problems, and that, until one could be found, the territorial staus quo on the PRC's borders would be duly observed. Yet, neither Peking's avowed willingness to tolerate existing conditions for a while longer nor its pledge not to use coercion to accomplish its goal meant, where it was concerned, that the frontiers with which modern history had saddled it were fixed and immutable. The Soviets too were thereby served notice that they would be well advised to mend their fences fast and not lull themselves into falsely believing that the recent shape of the southern perimeter of their Asian flank bore Peking's full endorsement.[9]

THE SOVIET RESPONSE:
COUNTERATTACK OR NEGOTIATE?

That left the next move up to Moscow. Thus far, the Soviets had gotten the Chinese to admit that they wanted to redraw the map of the PRC's international boundaries. However, Peking's reply also raised for them the question of what to do with the Chinese offer to sit down at the conference table.

Basically, the Kremlin could proceed in either of two directions. As a first alternative, it could move to counter the Chinese thesis on its merits, even if such an approach did meet with several difficulties of a doctrinal nature. For one, in the literature of the early Soviet phase, the Sino-Russian agreements lately attacked in Chinese quarters as "unequal treaties" likewise were frankly so denominated, and no Soviet commentator in those days tried to pretend that the terms of these documents were won by the tsarist diplomatic circles through honorable means.[10] Next, certain official Soviet pronouncements of that period had adopted a similar tone and, in fact, erased any doubt that, in the opinion of their authors, the conventions falling into the present category were, for that very reason, voidable at the discretion of the signatories. The Declaration of the Council of People's

Commissars of the Russian Soviet Federated Socialist Republic
(RSFSR) to the Chinese Nation and the Governments of Southern
and Northern China of July 25, 1919,[11] thus had already proclaimed
that "the Soviet government had renounced all the conquests made by
the tsarist government in depriving China of Manchuria and other
areas. Let the peoples themselves decide within the frontiers of
which state they want to be and what form of government they wish to
establish at home."

A little more than a year later, the Note from the People's
Commissariat of Foreign Affairs of the RSFSR to the Ministry of
Foreign Affairs of China, dated September 27, 1920, (commonly
known as the Karakhan Manifesto), again offered the Peking authorities a set of principles on which the Soviet regime was prepared to
institute negotiations at once toward normalizing contacts between
their countries.[12] The second message contained, inter alia, a
draft paragraph to the effect that "the government of the Russian
Soviet Federated Socialist Republic declares as without force all
treaties concluded by the former government of Russia with China,
renounces all seizures of Chinese territory, all Russian concessions
in China, and returns to China without compensation and forever all
that was rapaciously seized from her by the tsarist government and
the Russian bourgeoisie." Finally, it will be remembered, the Sino-Soviet accord of May 31, 1924, confirmed afresh, expressis verbis,
Moscow's apparent consent to review jointly with the Chinese "all
conventions, treaties, agreements, protocols, contracts, etc., concluded between the Government of China and the Tsarist Government
and to replace them with new treaties, agreements, etc., on the basis
of equality, reciprocity and justice, as well as the spirit of the Declarations of the Soviet Government of 1919 and 1920."

Technical explanations could, of course, minimize the substantive significance of these assorted public commitments, but their
derivative importance as a clear statement of official intent was
unassailable.[13] While the precise juridical weight of a unilateral
policy announcement emanating from a competent agency or of an
unfulfilled treaty clause continues to be a hotly debated issue, most
international law experts concede that both possess a modicum of
evidentiary value in determining the objectives sought by the party
or parties concerned and the subjacent conception of the rights
and duties involved. Still, with proper diligence, a respectable case
could be assembled in rebuttal of these various points.

Moscow's twin communications could be discounted, in the
way just mentioned, as mere positional papers, thereby raising
a serious question as to their ultimate juridical stature. Indeed,
solid historical precedent exists for such a view since, as far back
as 1923, the Soviet plenipotentiary representative in China, L. M.
Karakhan, already had occasion in the course of negotiations with

the Chinese government about, inter alia, the Soviet offer in its 1919 and 1920 communications to repudiate Russia's share of the Boxer indemnity, to remind the latter that: "The fact alone that the Chinese government has familiarized itself with their contents [that is, of the two notes] is insufficient to enable it to divest itself of the formal obligations imposed on it by the final protocol of 1901. . . . That the Chinese government knows of their contents [that is, of the two notes] does not yet give it any right to base its actions on their text. The Chinese government acquires rights arising from the principles of the Soviet declarations only in the event that these principles are formalized by a bilateral act possessed of international significance."[14] Furthermore, while the 1919 appeal specified elsewhere that the Soviet regime had from the start called on the Chinese side to hold conversations on the annulment of the treaty of 1896, the Peking protocol of 1901, and all the agreements with Japan from 1907 to 1916, none of which dealt with the territorial problem, on the latter score it remained singularly reticent.[15] The RSFSR's renunciation of the tsarist conquests in Manchuria was made explicit, but, for the rest, the text spoke only of "other areas" without designating what additional regions might fit the bill. Even then, the Soviets managed to append an extra qualification by gearing the whole matter to a prospective exercise in self-rule by the local population, a formula that in principle could work out to their advantage as much as to the benefit of the Chinese, save that in the meantime the situation was left up in the air. In the long run, this was bound to favor the cause of the power that retained physical mastery of the field, to wit, Soviet Russia.

The 1920 version quite obviously represented no more than a preliminary invitation to conduct discussions in the near future on a lengthy list of subjects of mutual interest, the frontier issue among them, and the featured reference to that item was equally indefinite with respect to its projected range and focus.[16] In neither instance, it must be emphasized, were those particular pacts which had contributed to drawing the modern outline of the Sino-Soviet border identified by name as scheduled for a thorough overhaul. Besides, the latest Soviet bid again produced no tangible results. The relevant provision of the treaty of May 31, 1924, which climaxed these exploratory efforts, brought no change in the existing pattern: while endorsing the familiar proposition that past agreements between the two nations were slated for proximate reassessment, its language carefully eschewed any indication of which of the conventions prescribing the geographic location of their functioning state boundary the signatories might here have had in mind;[17] in any event, the actual business of sifting through the accumulation of old documents, figuring out what to do with them, which to keep, which to discard,

THE SOVIET OFFENSIVE   51

which to amend, and which to replace entirely, was postponed until afterwards, when a special conference would address itself to that enormous task; the talks, when at last they materialized, left the job undone and the status quo lingered on undisturbed.[18]

To complete the picture, the Soviet attitude subsequently shifted. The revolutionary theories expounded at a young age gradually lost ground. A more conservative viewpoint emerged to which jurisprudential doctrine gave tongue by espousing the position that "the external frontiers of the territory inherited by the Soviet state through the process of historical and juridical succession to the former Russian empire were fixed by the frontier treaties of the empire in force on August 1, 1914."[19] So, since "the treaties. . .with Mongolia of November 5, 1921, and China of May 31, 1924, said nothing of alterations in the former. . .Chinese frontiers. . .the previous acts in force in 1914 still governed for the purposes of definition or redemarcation (in the event of damage) of the frontiers with. . . China and the Mongolian and Tannu-Tuvinian People's Republics established astride a portion of the Chinese frontier."[20] Or, in a slightly different version, "one of the species of treaties relating to territory concluded by tsarist Russia was treaties regulating boundary lines with neighboring states. Naturally, the new subject of international law—the Soviet state—could not but take into account the frontiers created by these treaties. In this instance, we speak less of recognition of the treaty itself than of the treaty frontiers."[21]

Or, to quote the most fully developed exposition of these concepts to date,

> the external frontiers of the territory inherited by the Union of Soviet Socialist Republics through the process of historical and juridical succession to the former Russian empire were not infrequently drawn by Russia's treaties concluded in the seventeenth, eighteenth, and nineteenth centuries. Among them, one can name the Treaty of Nerchinsk of 1689, the Treaties of Burin and Kiakhta of 1727, the Treaties of Aigun and Tientsin of 1858, the Treaty of Peking of 1860 and others in respect to the Far Eastern territories, . . .the conclusion of which had nothing to do with national self-determination in its contemporary sense. However, it would be practically impossible, and politically incorrect, and in no way justified to deny all significance to these acts of the past.
>
> Analysis of international practice demonstrates that some acts of the past are repudiated by the people, others retain their significance, in some cases the territorial status quo is reviewed, in others it is preserved.

> Inasmuch as today obsolete norms of law cannot serve as a basis for the solution of territorial questions, one must renounce those treaties and the legal foundations of the past stemming therefrom which run counter to the right of nations to self-determination. . . .
>
> Of the former international treaties, those acts keep their significance as legal bases for territorial delimitation which objectively correspond to the principle of national self-determination and, consequently, do not infringe upon the sovereign rights of the interested nations. All depends on the content with which history fills this or that legal form. That is why the old frontiers of the Russian empire with. . .China have remained unchanged. On the other side of the Chinese frontier the Mongolian and Tannu-Tuvinian People's Republics came into existence, and within the confines of the territory of the former Russian empire along the frontiers referred to arose on the basis of national self-determination the Central Asian national republics which became part of the Soviet Union. The old territorial delimitation won the recognition of the interested peoples and remained unchanged, with the exception of the Tuvinian sector, amended in connection with the voluntary merger in 1943 of the Tannu-Tuvinian People's Republic with the Soviet Union. The juridical title of the Soviet state to the territories located within the state frontiers of the Soviet Union rests on the voluntary and inviolable alliance of the free peoples of these territories based on the right of all nations to free self-determination guaranteed by the Constitution of the Soviet Union.[22]

What had started out as a purely de facto phenomenon—an accidental outgrowth of historical experience, qualitatively neutral in coloration—thus ended up invested with positive virtues and a distinct legal rationale. Whatever defects the end results of the historical process might have suffered from or, at least, whatever affirmative values they might have lacked were ostensibly cured or compensated for by the intercession of the canon of self-determination, to which Soviet spokesmen at this stage tended to attribute almost miraculous powers. Operating, as they seemed to, on the premise that "presumption of the coincidence of territorial supremacy with the sovereign will of the people must serve, from the viewpoint of contemporary international law, as the supreme juridical basis for territorial dominion,"[23] they saw the apparent acquiescence of the nationalities inhabiting the Soviet side of their Asian frontiers in

THE SOVIET OFFENSIVE 53

the status quo as prima facie validation of the present boundary line.

In sum, had the Soviets wanted to engage in legal polemics at this juncture, enough ammunition lay at hand from the annals of the intervening period—and, of course many new defenses have been articulated in recent years under the pressure of the ongoing dispute that could have been brought out of storage at the very outset[24]— to ensure a creditable performance on their part. Yet, as the subsequent record reveals, instead they held back and this unaccustomed "show of restraint" in turn bears looking into.

An excellent reason for not getting entangled in a legal debate was, of course, the bare fact that, from a jural standpoint, the substantive elements of tsarist Russia's territorial treaties with China still constituted the strongest single link in the Soviet case. However, no member of the Soviet hierarchy could contemplate with relish the thought of rallying to the defense of these agreements in a public forum, a thoroughly distasteful prospect for an acknowledged Communist in light of Marxist dogma. That in itself would inhibit any tendency to rely on the instrumentalities of the law in handling the affair. For that matter, the same can be said of the Chinese who in this respect here followed an identical line. Indeed, the PRC authorities then showed just as little inclination to file a formal legal brief and probably out of calculations not much different from those entertained by their opposites in the Kremlin. The impulse behind the expansion of the Middle Kingdom had, at its peak, been as imperialistic in inspiration as the impetus behind Russia's latter-day drive to the shores of the Pacific Ocean. To attempt to prove that China had good title to the remote border regions meant subscribing to the annexationist policies of the dynastic court vis-a-vis the alien peoples surrounding the Han nucleus of the empire, an approach no better suited to the ideological complexion of the new order than the notion of championing the tsarist regime's land acquisitions at the expense of Russia's weaker neighbors fitted the plans of its revolutionary successors.[25]

More generally, though, the observable behavior of both parties seemed to indicate a deliberate effort on their part to keep the dispute from becoming "juridified" and to prevent the current issue from hardening into an "object of legal contention." Consider these items. Khrushchev first raised the territorial question in a speech before his own parliament; true, his remarks were picked up at once by the mass media and widely disseminated, but they were not directly addressed to the Chinese "comrades" and did not amount to an official communication between the two governments. The Chinese riposte followed an even more roundabout path, taking the shape of an editorial in the Peking press replying to a statement released by the Communist party of the United States which had echoed Khrushchev's worst taunts. A face-to-face meeting was thus studiously avoided; the Soviet and PRC leaderships did not zero in on each other. Rather, they aired their views in front of a home audience or criticized a third party, letting the message reach its real destination by an intendedly circuitous route.

Nor was Peking's choice of Party channels to deliver its answer at all accidental. Khrushchev was discussing sundry aspects of the Soviet Union's foreign relations, including the Cuban crisis, and his comments on the PRC also dwelled on Communist China's dealings with various imperialist powers and India, that is, on select examples of state-to-state diplomacy. The question of the Sino-Soviet frontier, it will be recalled, did not enter into this picture, and the current conflict between Moscow and Peking was portrayed by the speaker essentially as a clash of opinions over doctrinal orthodoxy in matters of global strategy. Under these circumstances, there was nothing wrong with using a state occasion to analyze the situation and spell out the Soviet position on these topics. As against this, the Chinese response focused squarely on the problem of their shared boundary, but then sought to soften the blow by putting the whole affair in a Party context, with the dual aim apparently of emphasizing that, within the "socialist brotherhood," an item of this sort was not state business and also maintaining in this way a proper degree of balance in the intensity of the verbal counterthrust—escalation in one sector being compensated for by commensurate relaxation elsewhere. The important aspect is that the Chinese Communists were careful and able to keep the exchange of volleys from ballooning forthwith into an interstate confrontation.

The substantive contents of this strange "correspondence" reenforced the pattern. The concepts of "unequal treaties" and "national self-determination" both sprawl on the outskirts of the legal realm, straddling the thin line between law and politics. Conscious resort to such pseudolegal devices when superior legal tools were available again suggests a common concern with preventing the dialogue from slipping into the rigid format and legal patois of a "litigational contest." It also indicates each party's preoccupation with enhancing its own ideological stature by invoking a principle supplied with a certified "socialist" genealogy. In sum, if style accurately reflects the underlying purpose and if a subject's frame of mind can be ascertained from his chosen modus operandi, neither the Soviet nor the Chinese Communist regime played out the opening scene as though its vital interests were endangered. Nobody ran scared or even sounded worried enough to recite his legal rights, which generally happens when events take a serious turn.

This leaves us with the second alternative response to the PRC's March 1963 message—negotiations—and the perplexing question of what considerations held the Soviets back from exploring the promise inherent in the Chinese bid that all such issues be settled "peacefully" at the conference table "when conditions are ripe." Personal factors doubtless influenced Soviet official conduct on that score. Having cleverly conjured up the specter of Han imperial ambitions, Khrushchev must have been loath to exorcise that hardy ghost so soon. However, other, more routine impulses probably also had a role.

After all, on several previous occasions, similar expressions in diplomatic overtures emanating from Peking had led in short order to fruitful results. Boundary pacts had already been concluded with Burma and Nepal. On December 26, 1962, in the wake of the Sino-Indian hostilities and when the Sino-Soviet dispute was brewing, in a step that can only be described as a grand demonstrative gesture, a frontier treaty was signed with Mongolia, and Chinese commentators were quick to point out the universal lesson to be learned from this experience. The main message was beamed at the Indians, with assurances that:

> China's stand on the Sino-Indian boundary question is consistent with her stand on all other boundary questions: she has always striven for a settlement through peaceful negotiations. At the present time, the Chinese frontier guards, having been compelled to strike back in self-defense, have on their own initiative ceased fire along the entire border and are withdrawing. This fact provides still more incontrovertible evidence of China's sincere desire and unshakable stand for a peaceful settlement of the Sino-Indian boundary question.[26]

But, the moral of the story applied equally to the Soviets and the move was obviously aimed as much at Moscow as at New Delhi,[27] for elsewhere the Chinese waxed no less lyrical about how

> this swift settlement of the Sino-Mongolian boundary question and the successful signing of a boundary treaty provides a fine example of the way socialist countries handle their mutual relations. It shows how fraternal socialist countries find the correct way to solve questions existing between them on the basis of Marxism-Leninism and proletarian internationalism and in accordance with the principles governing mutual rela-

tions between fraternal countries as laid down in the
Moscow Declaration of 1957 and the Moscow Statement of
1960. It shows how a reasonable solution can be secured
for outstanding questions through comradely, friendly
consultations. In solving their boundary question, the
Chinese and Mongolian Governments are acting not only
in the interests of the unity and solidarity of the Chinese
and Mongolian peoples, but also in the interests of the
unity and solidarity of the peoples of all socialist
countries.[28]

Finally, just before the People's Daily unleashed its broadside against the Communist party of the United States for repeating Khrushchev's anti-Chinese remarks, the PRC and Pakistan likewise reached a border accord; and the year had not yet expired when Afghanistan, too, joined the list.

In each instance, of course, the outcome owed a great deal to purely political motives. Chinese interest in putting an early and painless end to the border problem with Burma and Nepal was closely linked with the difficulties encountered in resolving the smoldering controversy over the correct shape of the Sino-Indian frontier.[29] Productive talks with these two countries would serve to isolate India, throw into sharp relief the PRC's ability to work out a reciprocally satisfactory arrangement with a pair of smaller neighbors as compared to India's apparent intransigence, and exert pressure on the Indian government also to come to terms. Again, the impact of the timely signature of border agreements with Mongolia and Pakistan transcended the narrow confines of the immediate agenda. The success of the enterprise, in addition to being expected to pry Mongolia from its pro-Moscow orientation and Pakistan from its allegiance to SEATO, was plainly calculated to convince both India and the Soviet Union of the wisdom of following suit and composing their border differences without further delay. Plus, these samples of constructive international behavior would help offset the poor impression created in the eyes of world public opinion by the perpetual dissension over the matter of the precise silhouette of the PRC's perimeter with the Soviet Union and India.

More apropos, however, is the fact that in the process the Chinese Communist hierarchy managed to evolve a standard diplomatic formula to which the opposite side was in every case so far quite willing to subscribe. Thus, the whole length of the joint frontier was retraced in minute detail. Although the contracting powers invariably professed to be guided in their labors by a wish to preserve the "traditional customary boundary line," their findings coincided in most particulars with the old version of their combined border, except for a few minor adjustments in some spots.[30] In redefining the site of the frontier, no attention was paid to the provisions of past border agreements. Indeed, the very existence of these tainted witnesses to a bygone age was systematically ignored and the lone citation of a treaty harking back to the "colonial epoch" merely fulfilled a reference function. With the entry into force of the latest accords, all previous conventions regulating the location of the corresponding sector of the border lapsed and thereafter any question arising in connection with the format of the frontier would be governed by the appropriate document bearing the names of the PRC representatives.

The official refrain is that the course of the negotiations leading up to the conclusion of each frontier pact was marked by the spirit of mutual understanding and mutual accommodation, cordial consultations, fairness, and reasonableness—expressions that convey the flavor of ad hoc compromise, practical expediency, pragmatic outlook, flexible posture, and opportune improvisation, in short, of proceedings untrammeled by punctilio and trivial technicalities. Legal rights were never mentioned. Chinese sources noted with hearty approval, for example, how "the Chinese and Nepalese Governments had agreed that, prior to the overall settlement of the boundary question, they would maintain the status quo and not make any territorial claims on each other as pre-conditions for negotiation."[31] The rigid ritual of the law, then, did not set the tone here; instead, we are told, the ancient art of friendly political bargaining dominated the scene and, in an animus of quid pro quo, accomplished the objective in record time.

The end picture sounded almost idyllic. The resulting agreements neatly favored the PRC's cosignatories: their state frontiers with the PRC remained virtually intact and, as an extra bonus, received formal endorsement from the current mainland regime. Peking, in turn, wound up with a series of agreements which, in a very real sense, erased whole slices of the historical past, together with its many unpleasant memories, and redated the PRC's border relations with the countries involved to start with a new era.

What prevented India and the Soviet Union from at least testing the possibilities of handling their business with Communist China in the same neat fashion? For one, the situation had since deteriorated so much that they probably felt that any such venture entailed an unwarranted amount of risk. This mistrust of Chinese intentions was compounded, in the Soviet case, by exasperation with the ideological "perversity" of the PRC leadership. Thus, to put the fate of their entire frontier with the PRC at stake in the hope that the Communist Chinese authorities would act as they had on earlier occasions and again accept a modus vivendi essentially sanctioning the hitherto operative boundary line called for willingness to take a gamble that the Soviet and Indian governments both apparently thought was excessive. Readiness to engage in unconditional discussions on the status of their respective frontiers with the PRC could be interpreted as an admission of doubt on the part of either as to the intrinsic validity of the effective border, a factor which, if the negotiations failed, might in fine gravely prejudice the Soviet Union's or India's title to the disputed areas. So, the Indians, rather unwisely, brought up their biggest legal guns and insisted on making a juridical case of the affair, unheeding of the endless complications, profound bitterness, and inevitable recriminations that a litigational approach tends to engender, and thereby only succeeded in blocking every avenue to a compromise arrangement that easily could have met nearly all their demands. The Soviets, equally lacking in perspicacity, sought refuge behind a heavy ideological barrage, and by coupling the issue with the ongoing doctrinal controversy just as badly reduced their chances for a quick settlement.

Second, the key to the solution of the border problem between the PRC and Burma, Nepal, Pakistan, Mongolia, and Afghanistan lay in Peking's consent to waive China's traditional claims to peripheral territories once incorporated into the Chinese empire or under its suzerainty. These nations did not object to being cast in the role of beneficiaries of Chinese bounty, judging that the material gains they derived from the deal were fully worth the psychological price they were required to pay and the cost, by any count, was not exorbitant. The Soviet Union and India, however, concerned with their image and prestige as great powers, seemingly concluded that they could not afford to "demean" their rank by allowing themselves to be publicly identified as recipients of Chinese liberality, especially on an item the importance of which was obvious to everybody. Saving "face" can be an expensive proposition; in this instance it probably was.

Communist China was, of course, playing a similar game vis-a-vis its smaller neighbors, and its tactics on that score toward India and the Soviet Union were influenced by comparable considerations. During their protracted debate with the Soviets on the subject of their common frontier, for example, at no point until March 1969 did the Chinese invoke the Soviet Declaration of 1919 or the 1920 Karakhan Manifesto, although the tenor of both documents would have strengthened their argument, presumably because the latter represented a unilateral gesture of generosity by the Kremlin to which they did not want to be indebted in any way. Peking preferred, without regard to profit, to defend its interests by relying on its own resources, rather than using evidence borrowed from Soviet diplomatic archives, in order to be able to dramatize the constancy of the PRC's title to the territory in question and its utter independence of any momentary aberration in the spectrum of Soviet foreign policy. And, even when

THE SOVIET OFFENSIVE

the mainland regime finally did refer to these texts,[32] it was not for the purpose of adducing some positive right accruing from their contents but merely to illustrate the inconsistency of Soviet behavior and to spotlight the extent to which the attitude of the current Soviet leadership was at variance with the spirit of Lenin's "great testament."

NOTES

1. <u>Zasedaniya Verkhovnogo Soveta SSSR shestogo sozyva, vtoraya sessiya (10-13 dekabrya 1962g.), stenograficheskii otchet</u>, Moscow, 1963, pp. 492-93; <u>The Present International Situation and the Foreign Policy of the Soviet Union</u>, Report presented by N. S. Khrushchev, First Secretary of the Communist Party of the Soviet Union and Chairman of the USSR Council of Ministers, to the Supreme Soviet, in a joint session of the Soviet of the Union and the Soviet of Nationalities, in the Great Palace of the Kremlin, on December 12th, 1962 (Soviet Booklet No. 104), London, December 1962, pp. 19-20.

2. <u>Zasedaniya Verkhovnogo Soveta SSSR</u>, p. 504; <u>The Present International Situation and the Foreign Policy of the Soviet Union</u>, p. 29.

3. How badly Sino-Soviet relations have since deteriorated may be judged, for instance, from the tone of the recent critique of the book by Neville Maxwell, <u>India's China War</u>, 2nd ed., London: Pantheon, 1971, published by N. S. Karinin, in <u>Problemy Dalnego Vostoka</u>, 1974, No. 1, pp. 159-64, in which the reviewer faults virtually every attempt by Maxwell to present the Chinese view of the conflict's origins and sides completely with India's position in the dispute.

4. A. Kruchinin, V. Olgin, <u>Territorial Claims of Mao Tse-tung: History and Modern Times</u>, Moscow, n.d., pp. 18-19.

5. <u>The Worker</u>, New York, January 13, 1963; <u>Political Affairs</u>, 1963, No. 2, pp. 1-6; excerpted in D. J. Doolin, <u>Territorial Claims in the Sino-Soviet Conflict, Documents and Analysis</u>, Stanford, Hoover Institution Studies No. 7, 1965, pp. 28-29.

6. English translation in <u>Peking Review</u>, 1963, Nos. 10-11, pp. 58-62; <u>A Comment on the Statement of the Communist Party of the U.S.A.</u>, Peking, 1963; excerpts in A. Dallin (ed.), <u>Diversity in International Communism, A Documentary Record, 1961-1963</u>, New York: Columbia University Press, 1963, pp. 809-13.

7. <u>A Comment on the Statement of the Communist Party of the U.S.A.</u>, pp. 12-14.

8. V. M. Khvostov, "Kitaiskii 'schet po reestru' i pravda istorii," <u>Mezhdunarodnaya zhizn'</u>, 1964, No. 10, p. 23.

9. N. Maxwell, "Simmering Dispute along the Sino-Soviet Border," Times (London), Sept. 30, 1968, p. 9: "The basic Chinese position was that the boundaries must be renegotiated. The old, unequal treaties, reminders of China's generations of humiliation, must be replaced by new boundary agreements negotiated between equals. Until this was done, China would regard the Sino-Russian boundaries as not formally delimited. But in the meantime she would respect the status quo—and Peking made it clear that an insistence on renegotiating the boundaries was not at all the same thing as an insistence on changing them. Bitterly as the old injustice of the unequal treaties was resented by the Chinese, they were prepared to accept the boundaries thus established as a fact of life. The lost territories were gone for good. As Mr. Chou En-lai told the late Mr. Nehru in the same context: 'China has [still] a vast expanse of territory, more than half of which is sparsely populated,' and therefore had no interest in an irredentist quest for living space."

10. For example, V. P. Savvin, Vzaimootnosheniya tsarskoi Rossii a Kitaem, 1619-1917. Moscow, 1930; V. Andersen, "Neravnopravnye dogovora Tsarskoi Rossii s Kitaem v XIX veke," Borba klassov, 1936, No. 9, pp. 102-12. For a brief survey of the changing attitudes in Russian and Soviet historical literature on the status of Russia's early agreements with China and a citation of the major pertinent works, see L. G. Beskrovnyi's review of Russko-kitaiskie otnosheniya v XVII veke, Moscow, 1972, Vol. 2, in Problemy Dalnego Vostoka, 1974, No. 1, pp. 155-56.

11. Izvestiya, Aug. 26, 1919; Dokumenty vneshni politiki SSSR, Moscow, 1958, Vol. 2, pp. 221-23.

12. Dokumenty vneshnei politiki SSSR, Moscow, 1959, Vol. 3, pp. 213-16; Sovetsko-kitaiskie otnosheniya, 1917-1957, sbornik dokumentov, Moscow, 1959, pp. 51-53.

13. Today Soviet authors consistently refer to various pronouncements by Lenin (for example, V. I. Lenin, Polnoe sobranie sochinenii, Vol. 35, p. 20; Vol. 45, p. 303) and his Commissar for Foreign Affairs, G. V. Chicherin (see, G. V. Chicherin, Stat'i i rechi po voprosam mezhdunarodnoi politiki, Moscow, 1961, pp. 58-59; E. A. Grigor'eva, E. D. Kostikov, "Spekulyatsii maoistov ponyatiem 'neravnopravnyi dogovor'," Problemy Dalnego Vostoka, 1975, No. 1, p. 56), to the effect that secret treaties only had been unilaterally annulled by the Soviet government, that the Soviet authorities had never repudiated in toto all the treaties concluded by the tsarist regime and the Provisional government and that, apart from the treaties annulled by the Decree on Peace, the fate of all the other treaties had to be resolved on an ad hoc basis through direct negotiations between the interested parties. As regards China, the treaties expressly identified by the Soviet government as susceptible of

cancellation by mutual consent were the treaty of 1896, the Peking protocol of 1901, and all the agreements with Japan from 1907 to 1916. None of these, Russian spokesmen emphasize, touched on the border issue nor were any of the treaties that did deal with the frontier question <u>secret</u> treaties. See, for example, V. M. Khvostov, <u>op. cit.</u>, p. 27; L. Beskrovnyi, S. Tikhvinskii, V. Khvostov, "K istorii formirovaniya russko-kitaiskoi granitsy," <u>Mezhdunarodnaya zhizn'</u>, 1972, No. 6, p. 28; L. G. Beskrovnyi, A. L. Narochnitskii, "K istorii vneshnei politiki Rossii na Dalnem Vostoke v XIX veke," <u>Voprosy istorii</u>, 1974, No. 6, p. 36; A. Kruchinin, V. Olgin, <u>op. cit.</u>, pp. 88-90; F. Nikolaev, "Kak v Pekine falsifitsiruyut istoriyu," <u>Mezhdunarodnaya zhizn'</u>, 1973, No. 4, p. 40; O. B. Borisov, B. T. Koloskov, <u>Sovetsko-kitaiskie otnosheniya 1945-1970, kratkii ocherk,</u> Moscow, 1971, p. 440; E. A. Grigor'eva, E. D. Kostikov, <u>op. cit.</u>, pp. 51-52, 55-56.

The legal effect of these public statements, however, is open to doubt. As far as the Chinese were concerned, the explicit language of the diplomatic communications received from Moscow governed the subject matter and these documents either used sweeping terms such as "all treaties, agreements, and so on" or were ambiguous about what conventions they had in mind and created the impression that indeed the entire accumulation of past treaties was being abrogated or would in due course be cancelled. In light of the grandiolquent or ambivalent phraseology that hinted at a tabula rasa situation, the Chinese were under no obligation to check what other views were meanwhile being expressed by responsible Soviet figures in order to put the memoranda into context and interpret their contents in the spirit of assorted other material, much of which was in fact not even available to them.

14. Memorandum of the Extraordinary Plenipotentiary Representative of the USSR in China, L. M. Karakhan, to the Chinese Government of December 13, 1923, in <u>Sovetsko-kitaiskie otnosheniya</u>, <u>1917-1957</u>, pp. 71-73.

15. The Soviet regime apparently took that approach from the very beginning. According to A. Kruchinin, V. Olgin, <u>op. cit.</u>, p. 89, for instance, already "as far back as 1917, the Soviet government had offered to hold negotiations with China on annulling not all treaties but only the one concluded in 1896, the Peking Protocol of 1901, and all treaties with Japan from 1907 to 1916."

16. An interesting attempt is made by A. Kruchinin, V. Olgin, <u>op. cit.</u>, pp. 88-89, to explain away the sweeping language of the 1920 Manifesto and its singular silence on what specific Russo-Chinese agreements qualified for annulment in accordance with its proposals. They contend that "because of previous statements of the Soviet government on treaties specifically subject to annulment, no

further mention of them was made [in the 1920 Note], although it was obviously those treaties that were meant."

In the first place, such an interpretation is really not "obvious" from the tenor of the document itself. In the second place, once again, it was not incumbent on the Chinese either to ascertain unarticulated Soviet intentions in light of the clear and express language of the written instrument or seek additional explanations on what might have been meant when the written communication looked quite definite and did not seem to require extra elucidation as to the sense of its message.

17. An interesting and technically sound argument is advanced by E. A. Grigor'eva, E. D. Kostikov, op. cit., pp. 56-57, to the effect that "already the fact alone that in the agreement, besides clauses on the necessity of replacing treaties concluded earlier by new ones and the annulment of a number of principles of Russo-Chinese relations of the past, is inserted an article which contains the consent of the parties to perform a verification [emphasis in the original] of the frontier—an ordinary technical operation, performed from time to time by all countries, without any indication that after this verification the parties must conclude a new frontier treaty—means, in practical terms, that the parties considered the frontier quite just and reasonable."

It should be added, however, that while the language of the agreement does, stricto sensu, indeed lend itself to this type of legal interpretation, the historical record shows that the Chinese government did not share this point of view. According to the Russians themselves, (A. Kruchinin, V. Olgin, op. cit., p. 90):

> At the negotiations in Peking in 1925-1926, envisaged by the agreement of May 31, 1924, the representatives of the Peking ruling militarist clique, in an effort to make use of nationalistic aspirations for struggling with the revolutionary forces of South China, declared that they did not recognize the treaties which determined the delineation of the Soviet-China border and claimed the whole territory, from the Maritime and Amur areas almost up to lake Baikal, to be Chinese.
> In a letter to People's Commissar Chicherin, ambassador Karakhan stressed that "the Chinese raise this question not so much in the hope of getting anything as in an effort to show that they are good patriots." The negotiations were adjourned for holidays on the initiative of the Chinese delegation, and, in view of internal political changes in China, were not resumed.

THE SOVIET OFFENSIVE 63

Whatever the Soviet appreciation of Chinese motives at the conference, the fact remains that the formula in question did give rise to conflicting official points of view and the Soviet thesis, though tenable, is by no means the only one possible, as their own experience in 1925-26 graphically demonstrated.

18. A. Kruchinin, V. Olgin, op. cit., pp. 89-90, point out that in his note of July 13, 1920, Karakhan, Deputy People's Commissar for Foreign Affairs, informed the Chinese authorities that: "The government of the USSR, of its own accord, and on its own initiative, addressed the Chinese people as far back as 1919 with a declaration which stated its readiness to abolish all unequal treaties concluded between China and tsarist Russia. The government of the USSR had realized its declarations in the treaty of 1924." They conclude that "consequently, refernce to Karakhan's note of September 27, 1920, is not valid."

The legal soundness both of Karakhan's original assertion and the authors' current extrapolation is extremely questionable. A unilateral declaration by one party to an agreement that it considered the purpose of the agreement fulfilled in the face of the other signatory's insistence to the contrary is simply a self-serving argument and not an objective determination of the true legal state of affairs. Furthermore, a claim that the intentions of the agreement were satisfied when the conference called to translate the general terms of the agreement into concrete arrangements produced no results represents a very unusual, to say the least, approach to the relevant norms of international public law. Lastly, perhaps "the government of the USSR had realized its declarations in the treaty of 1924," but certainly the Chinese thought otherwise and, as was indicated in the previous footnote, had officially advanced a totally different interpretation of the treaty's intent with regard, specifically, to the frontier issue. Under the circumstances, no binding value can automatically be attached to one side's adversary statement on the purported meaning of a bilateral agreement in the face of a contrary interpretation by the other party. Going by the record and applying the standard norms of international law, a much safer conclusion would in fact be that the aims of the 1924 treaty were not realized, leaving the status quo in force which may indeed have been what the Soviets privately had in mind from the start. But the 1924 treaty itself does not vindicate the Soviet position; only the failure to follow up on its provisions can be cited in defense of the status quo, a result of omission or default on the treaty and not a positive outgrowth of the treaty proper.

19. V. N. Durdenevskii, "Sovetskaya territoriya v aktakh mezhdunarodnogo prava za 30 let (1917-1947gg.)," Sovetskoe gosudarstvo i pravo, 1947, No. 12, p. 58.

20. Ibid., p. 62.

21. M. M. Avakov, Pravopreemstvo Sovetskogo gosudarstva, Moscow, 1961, p. 88.

22. Yu. G. Barsegov, Territoriya v mezhdunarodnom prave, Moscow, 1958, pp. 118-20.

23. Ibid., pp. 120-21. Cf., V. S. Shevtsov, National Sovereignty and the Soviet State, Moscow, 1974, p. 85: "International treaties objectively based on the principle of the self-determination of nations retain their legal importance. The borders between the Soviet Union and Iran, Afghanistan, and China are based on treaties signed by tsarist Russia." In the same vein, V. M. Khvostov, op. cit., p. 22; A. Kruchinin, V. Olgin, op. cit., p. 87; I. P. Blishchenko, Antisovetizm i mezhdunarodnoe pravo, Moscow, 1968, p. 74.

24. To cite just two such defenses: 1) O. B. Borisov, B. T. Koloskov, op. cit., p. 271, revive, inter alia, the old chestnut about the Soviet-Chinese frontier following natural landmarks; and, 2) an interesting and ingenious thesis has gradually been developed by Soviet authors to the effect that the Treaty of Nerchisk of 1689 was an aggressive, unequal treaty dictated by the Manchu rulers to the Russian court and unlawfully depriving Russia of its peacefully acquired possessions in the Amur-Ussuri valley which had never previously belonged to the Chinese state. Therefore, the subsequent treaties which engineered the reversion of most of these lost territories to Russia are said to have righted an earlier wrong, cancelled the effects of an anterior unequal treaty, restored the original state of affairs, and vindicated Russia's legitimate rights to most of the lands which it had been compelled to cede by the Nerchinsk treaty. For elaborate articulations of this theme, see V. M. Khvostov, op. cit., pp. 21-27; L. Beskrovnyi, S. Tikhvinskii, V. Khvostov, op. cit., pp. 14-29; P. I. Kabanov, Amurskii vopros, Blagoveshchensk, 1959; P. T. Yakovleva, Pervyi russko-kitaiskii dogovor 1689g., Moscow, 1958; L. G. Beskrovnyi, in Problemy Dalnego Vostoka, 1974, No. 1, pp. 155-59; A. Kruchinin, V. Olgin, op. cit., pp. 50-78; V. S. Myasnikov, Russian-Chinese Relations in the Seventeenth Century (documents and materials), dittoed.

25. For example, V. M. Khvostov, op. cit., p. 25, criticizing Chinese claims to the territory on the left bank of the Amur River based on the presence of Chinese picket lines in that area and the collection of tribute from the local population, flatly denies the validity of the argument on the grounds that:

> The collection of tribute and the dislocation of pickets were the result of predatory raids by the Chinese troops on foreign lands. Quite obviously, from the point of view of a Communist legal outlook these predatory aggressive

actions of the Ching monarchy lasting many centuries could not create any Chinese rights to the territories of the peoples of Central Asia. One cannot seriously speak of such kind of "rights."

The author does not seem aware that the process of Russian penetration and conquest of Siberia could be described in roughly similar terms. At any rate, he sees the picture differently, of course, and cites other features which presumably redeem Russia's record in that respect: for example, the concept of "proletarian acquisition" of Siberia, namely, that the operation was largely the work of "common folk" and not a state-militaristic venture as in the case of the Manchus; the factor of local settlement and economic development, in contrast with sporadic Manchu raids and brutal depredations; the notion of "proletarian prescription," that is, prolonged economic acquisition of the land and its resources by the working classes, independently of state policy; Manchu China's character as a more reactionary and no less aggressive power than tsarist Russia; and so forth.

26. "The Sino-Mongolian Boundary Treaty: Its Significance," PR, 1962, No. 52, p. 5.

27. On the topic of Chinese attempts to bracket the Soviet Union and India in connection with the unresolved boundary issues, see V. S. Olgin, "Ekspansionizm v pogranichnoi politike Pekina," Problemy Dalnego Vostoka, 1975, No. 1, p. 36, citing IX s'ezd Kommunisticheskoi Partii Kitaya (dokumenty), Peking, 1969, p. 36; A. Kruchinin, V. Olgin, op. cit., p. 8, citing Lin Piao's statement at the 9th Congress to the effect that only the questions of the PRC's border "with the Soviet Union and India have not yet found a solution."

Note, in particular, the statement by V. S. Myasnikov, A. G. Yakovlev, in Kitai segodnya, Moscow, 1969: ". . .the prompt conclusion of the negotiations concerning the frontier of the PRC with the MPR which had dragged on for almost five years was intended to serve as a practical confirmation of Peking's peaceful disposition and at the same time set a precedent for posing the question of review of the frontier with the other socialist countries, specifically—with the USSR." Also, Ong Cebeng, "Recognition of Mongolia," Independent Formosa, 1966, Nos. 5-6, p. 10.

28. "The Sino-Mongolian Boundary Treaty," p. 5.

29. Viz., A. Kruchinin, V. Olgin, op. cit., pp. 9-10; V. Olgin, op. cit., pp. 36-37. For critical Soviet comments on Chinese performance even after the signature of appropriate frontier treaties, see I. Shchedrov, "Provalivshayasya provokatsiya," Pravda, Feb. 6, 1974, and V. A. Krivtsov, "Maoizm i velikokhanskii shovinizm kitaiskoi burzhuazii," Problemy Dalnego Vostoka, 1974, No. 1, pp. 74-87.

30. Interestingly enough, this phenomenon which many Western observers see as evidence of Chinese reasonableness in solving border problems with their neighbors has also come under attack from Soviet commentators. The gist of the criticism is that the Chinese willingness to endorse a boundary line essentially identical with the one previously in operation after having for many years insisted that large pieces of territory across the existing boundary historically belonged to China demonstrates the perversity of the PRC leadership in fanning a crisis situation on its borders for ulterior political motives and without any regard to the intrinsic merits of the territorial claims advanced, only to drop the issue when it suited its purposes. In short, the PRC's ultimate readiness to accept a modus vivendi largely based on the status quo is perceived as a reckless indulgence in "cartographical aggression" and even "cartographical war" without any genuine commitment to the objective value of the claims being made which are then casually abandoned at a politically opportune moment.

31. Mao Sun, "Final Settlement of Sino-Nepalese Boundary Questions, D. Giri in Peking," PR, 1963, No. 4, p. 10.

32. Information Department of the Chinese Foreign Ministry, "Chenpao Island Has Always Been Chinese Territory," PR, 1969, No. 11, pp. 14-15; New York Times, Mar. 12, 1969, p. 16; Statement of the PRC Government, May 24, 1969, China Reconstructs, 1969, No. 7, Suppl., p. 4.

3

STALEMATE

A pause on this front followed the first flurry of verbal exchanges. Both capitals used the lull to advantage to launch confidential probes reportedly inspired by a concern to bring the polemics to an early and peaceful close. Thus, many years later, Russian sources revealed how "during that period the Soviet Government took quite a number of constructive steps to avert the sharpening of border friction, to lessen tension. With these aims, the Soviet Government on May 17, 1963, proposed to the PRC Government that bilateral consultations be held between our states."[1] The official story did not discuss the terms of the Soviet offer, but it has since been disclosed that the Russians in this case pursued their standard policy of serving notice of readiness to explore means of "defining the border more precisely in certain areas,"[2] that is, to engage in ad hoc redemarcation of individual stretches of the boundary line which, for some reason, required a fresh physical checkup. PRC spokesmen countered with their own version, according to which "on August 23, 1963, the Chinese Government put forward to the Soviet Government a six-point proposal for maintaining the status quo of the boundary and averting conflicts,"[3] which, inter alia, suggested that:

> The two sides pledge themselves to maintain the status quo of the boundary and not to push forward the line of actual control on the boundary in any way.
> The two sides pledge themselves to avert conflicts, and under no circumstances shall the frontier and other personnel of either side use force or the threat of force against the personnel of the other side or fire on the other side.
> In areas where a river forms the boundary, the frontier patrol route of each side shall not cross the main channel of navigable rivers.
> The present agreement does not concern questions of the ownership of territory. Differences of opinion between

the two sides on the boundary question shall be left for settlement by the two governments in the boundary negotiations.[4]

Interestingly enough, both sides have implied that their particular initiative deserved the credit for paving the way for the convening of the 1964 border talks, although at the time neither betrayed a desire to advertise its efforts, nor does the known record indicate that the overtures met with any measure of success at that juncture.[5] The reason for the failure of Moscow's bid is fairly obvious, since the kind of operation the Russians envisaged was too narrow in scope to suit the Chinese. The latter had repeatedly made it clear that they would not lend themselves to a mere resurvey of the existing boundary line, with perhaps a few minor adjustments in the current alignment, and its practical demarcation in situ, thereby leaving the status quo virtually unchanged and the Soviets in actual possession of the disputed terrain.

The main hitch in the Chinese plan, as far as the Soviets were concerned, was probably the business of everybody staying on his own flank of the main channel of navigable rivers where these formed the boundary. Such a move would essentially have called for a Soviet pullback and would amount to a "de facto abandonment" of the numerous islands across the _thalweg_ in both the Amur and Ussuri Rivers which the Soviets considered their territory and over which they apparently exercised effective control. To be sure, the Chinese did take the precaution of confirming that none of these preliminary steps would affect the ownership of the contested areas, which would ultimately be resolved through official negotiations and by mutual agreement. Nevertheless, from the Soviet standpoint, even a limited compromise harbored certain dangers: first, the withdrawal alone could be, and if the controversy dragged on, in the end definitely would be construed as some sort of admission by the Russians that their claim to these islands was debatable and, to that extent, would becloud Soviet title to these pieces of land; and, second, despite the juridical reservation about the matter of final ownership, the plain willingness to exert less than full sovereignty over these bits of territory for the duration of the quarrel could already be interpreted as a tacit acknowledgment that the matter was in doubt and thus serve further to undermine Soviet title to this soil.[6]

PRC SHATTERS PUBLIC SILENCE OVER SINKIANG, 1963

Regardless of what went on behind the scenes, in the public forum the brief silence was rudely shattered on September 6, 1963, with the publication of a "Comment on the Open Letter [of July 14, 1963] of the Central Committee of the CPSU" by the editorial departments of People's Daily and Red Flag.[7] Analyzing the recent background of the Moscow-Peking conflict, the authors at one point censored the Soviet side for the first time for having "provoked troubles on the Sino-Soviet border"[8] and, elsewhere, took the "leaders of the CPSU" to task for having

> in April and May 1962. . .used their organs and personnel in Sinkiang, China, to carry out large-scale subversive activities in the Ili region and enticed and coerced several tens of thousands of Chinese citizens into going to the Soviet Union. The Chinese Government lodged repeated protests and made repeated representations, but the Soviet government refused to repatriate these Chinese citizens on the pretext of "the sense of Soviet legality" and "humanitarianism." To this day this incident remains unsettled. This is indeed an astounding event, unheard of in the relations between socialist countries.[9]

Public mention of "troubles on the Sino-Soviet border" was new. Unfortunately, the Chinese source gave no details on the extent and location of the alleged "troubles" that would permit an assessment of the nature of the difficulties and the gravity of the situation. The present label could cover anything from an isolated border crossing to a local armed clash and, in concrete terms, the two types of occurrence lie very far apart.

The imputation that the Soviets had a finger or even a few fingers in the Sinkiang pie is probably justified.[10] While not immediately connected with rival territorial claims,[11] the episode at least officially identified one major arena of political competition. At any rate, the Soviets stood formally charged by their allies with flagrantly violating PRC sovereignty in Sinkiang. On the other hand, it should also be remembered that Peking's policies in that remote province had met with the spontaneous resistance of the native population more than once before and that the Chinese, casting around for a convenient scapegoat, were not at all averse to blaming the Soviets for their predicament.

For some obscure reason, Moscow did not respond at the time to the substance of the PRC allegations. Perhaps Sinkiang was too sensitive a topic for the Soviets to get involved in open polemics about what was going on over there: after all, we know that this is where the first serious border confrontation—the so-called Buz-Aigyr incident—happened in 1960, and very likely the Soviet role in Sinkiang's affairs was sufficiently questionable to convince them to skirt the issue lest a public debate bare additional embarrassing information about their activities in the area. Much later, however, Soviet secondary sources did try to counter Peking's accusations with their own elaborate version of what transpired on that occasion and, not surprisingly, they concentrated on the theme of the PRC government's practice of Han chauvinism and racial and cultural oppression and discrimination vis-a-vis the local ethnic minority, while painting the Soviet Union in suitably benevolent colors as a champion and protector of the beleaguered native population.

THE SOVIET SIDE TO THE SINKIANG ISSUE

According to the Soviet account, in the spring of 1962 the inhabitants of Sinkiang staged a mass exodus to Soviet territory to escape from economic hardships and national persecution from which they were suffering as a result of the policies initiated by the Maoist authorities. At first, the Soviets say, the PRC Deputy Foreign Minister called the phenomenon an "unfortunate event," but subsequently Peking changed its tune and blamed the whole thing on "the subversive activities of the Soviet authorities." The Soviets trace the roots of the problem to the fact that a few hundred thousand people born in Russia (principally Kazakhs and Uighurs) had at various times settled down in Sinkiang (primarily during the civil war in Russia). By virtue of the Decrees of the USSR Supreme Soviet of November 10, 1945, and January 20, 1946, about 120,000 of them formally registered as Soviet citizens and received Soviet permits to live abroad; but many in their midst for different reasons did not receive proper documents, although under the terms of Soviet legislation they had not lost Soviet citizenship.

At the outset, the attitude of the PRC officialdom toward this contingent was friendly; however, conditions subsequently deteriorated. Starting in 1958-59, Soviet citizens permanently residing in Sinkiang saw their property, legal, and other rights curtailed, while dismissals from jobs in state institutions and enterprises became commonplace, and persecutions for petty infractions increased in frequency. The personnel of Chinese institutions treated Soviet citizens rudely, rejecting the simplest requests, ridiculed their national mores and customs, and prohibited the use of their mother tongue. Simultaneously, in the beginning of 1962, the local authorities in Sinkiang ceased almost entirely to issue exit permits to the Soviet Union to Soviet citizens wanting to return home.

As a result, we are told, in the spring of 1962 a swarm of people who were no longer able to put up with the harsh living conditions, famine, national discrimination, persecution, and anti-Soviet debauchery fled spontaneously to the safety of Soviet territory and just between April 22 and early June 1962, 67,000 souls illegally crossed the frontier. The Chinese tried to blame the Soviet authorities for "welcoming those who violated" the border. In reply, the Soviets sent a note on April 29, 1962, which rejected the PRC charges and pointed out that the crossings of the frontier occurred from the Chinese side, under the eyes of the PRC authorities who therefore ought to take appropriate measures to stem the tide. Indeed, Soviet sources have since embroidered on this version by claiming that the PRC officials, realizing that recourse to force in this case would only compromise them, soon switched to a different tactic and actually abetted the departures. The authorities in Kuldja and Chuguchak, so the story goes, informed the citizens demanding permission to leave for the Soviet Union that they did not require visas and could simply cross the frontier. A system was even organized for the sale of tickets for highway travel to border points and the dispatch of luggage by postal conveyances. Toward the end of May 1962, some 10-20 trucks loaded with 40-50 persons each left daily from Kuldja alone. The passengers descended a few kilometers from the border and continued their trip on foot. While so engaged, the Chinese allegedly insisted that the Soviets employ brute force against persons seeking to cross the frontier in the expectation that if the refugees were met with bullets and bayonets and compelled to return to the PRC, the Soviets would incur the eternal hatred of these unfortunate folk.

Reportedly, the Soviet government persistently sought ways of amicably resolving the ensuing problem. The fugitives were urged to return to the PRC and, if they then wished to emigrate to the Soviet Union, to do so through established channels. The Soviet government repeatedly invited the competent PRC agencies to send representatives to talk to the refugees, but they refused, presumably because they understood full well that not many individuals would care to go back. A few did, chiefly people who had left numerous relatives behind. Nevertheless, the Chinese demanded that all the inhabitants of Sinkiang who had escaped to the Soviet Union be forcibly returned, even under threat of resort to arms, and at the same time stated they would not accept those who had volunteered for repatriation. The Soviet government would not consent physically to expel people who had fled for their lives, the bulk of them old folk, women, and children.

Diplomatic messages, larded with mutual recriminations, flew back and forth. The PRC Ministry of Foreign Affairs asserted that the Soviets had "prepared and organized the mass crossing," that Sinkiang was in imminent danger of "serious subversive activity by the Soviet Union," and the like. The Soviet government denied the truth of these statements and spelled out its own position on the course of events in Sinkiang, especially in connection with the widespread flight of the local population to Soviet soil. The PRC leadership reiterated its earlier claims, added that the Soviets were also responsible for having provoked the bloody incidents in Kuldja in the spring of 1962 (Moscow, in turn, maintained that the Chinese had here deliberately staged a pogrom of the non-Han elements among the population which entailed heavy loss of human life)[12] and demanded once again that all the refugees forthwith be restored to PRC jurisdiction, while continuing to reject the suggestion that they dispatch representatives to persuade the fugitives to retrace their steps.

In the end, the Chinese themselves were obliged to acquiesce in the desire of Soviet citizens and people born in Russia to leave for the Soviet Union. In September 1962, the PRC Ministry of Foreign Affairs asked the Soviet government to allow entry into the Soviet Union through a simplified procedure individuals who wanted to move there. Acceding to the request, the Soviet authorities introduced a temporary program of visa-less immigration to the Soviet Union from the PRC of Soviet citizens and members of their families. From October 15, 1962, to May 1, 1963, more than 46,000 souls availed themselves of this opportunity to quit Sinkiang for the Soviet Union. Eventually, the Soviet government found it necessary to propose to the PRC authorities that the normal visa regime be restored, for the flow of repatriates continued unabated and the influx badly strained the capacity of local resources to provide all concerned with adequate living space and employment.[13]

The accuracy of the respective scripts cannot be verified and, apart from noting that each side had an explanation of the occurrence which, quite naturally, served to put it in the best possible light, no conclusion can be drawn at this juncture concerning the authenticity of the competing versions. From the standpoint of style and format, however, the important feature is that the Peking regime's bill of indictment of September 6, 1963, was still careful to treat the matter as an interparty affair. Hence, the next Soviet move—in the guise of a "government statement" released on September 21, 1963—marked a significant departure in that regard.

THE SOVIET POLICY PAPER, 1963

The ostensible reason for the switch in polemical media was that, upon acquainting itself with the contents of the "statement by a spokesman of the Chinese government" against the treaty banning nuclear weapon tests in the atmosphere, in outer space, and under water, circulated in Peking on September 1, 1963—to which the

September 21 communication was a response—Moscow now discovered that

> on this occasion, too, a government statement is being used mainly in order to slander the Communist Party of the Soviet Union (CPSU) and the other Communist parties in connection with a wide range of questions on which the leadership of the Communist Party of China (CPC) has differences with the international Communist movement.[14]

On most of the subjects touched upon in the Soviet policy paper, recourse to official channels was appropriate enough, since they involved diverse aspects of international diplomacy. This applied to the topic of the Sino-Indian border hostilities as well, an item on which the Soviets firmly clung to the old line that "we consider that in frontier disputes, especially in a dispute of the type of the Chinese-Indian clash, one should adhere to the Leninist views according to which it is possible to settle any frontier problem without resorting to armed force, granted that both sides desire to do so."[15] It is where the Kremlin then embarked on a discussion of the growing friction along the Sino-Soviet boundary in the same conceptual frame of reference that the element of novelty emerged. For, with this step, the Soviets virtually raised the issue to a state level, except that they endeavored to make it look as though their Chinese colleagues were liable for this adverse turn of events because they had purportedly instituted the offensive practice of expounding on ideological themes in government documents and left the Soviets no choice save to retaliate in kind.

Moscow's assertion was unfounded, needless to say, since that was precisely the sort of error top PRC circles seemed determined not to commit, and to date they had managed to avoid the trap. Yet, none of this prevented the Soviets from premeditatedly trying to saddle the Chinese with full responsibility for stirring up a crisis on the PRC-USSR boundary, which helps explain the strident tones of the accusations hurled by the Kremlin to the effect that

> in recent years, on her borders with neighboring states, the Chinese side has been stooping to acts of a nature which gives us reason to think that the government of the People's Republic of China is departing, on this question, more and more from Leninist positions. The leaders of the People's Republic of China are deliberately concentrating the people's attention on frontier problems, artificially fanning nationalist passions and dislike for other peoples.

To Peking's version of the causes of the border strife, Moscow opposed its own interpretation, recounting how

> since 1960, Chinese servicemen and civilians have been systematically violating the Soviet frontier. In the one year of 1962, more than 5,000 violations of the Soviet frontier from the Chinese side have been recorded. Attempts are also being made to "develop" some parts of Soviet territory without permission.
>
> One Chinese citizen who crossed the border had written instructions from the People's Committee of the Heilun Ch'iang province, which said: "When fish are being caught on the disputed islands of the Amur and the Ussuri, the Soviet border guards often demand that our fishermen leave these islands. We propose that the catching of fish on the disputed islands be continued and that the Soviet border guards be told that these islands belong to China, and that the border is being violated by them, not by us." And further: ". . . our fishermen are not to be removed from these islands in any circumstances. We imagine that, in view of the friendly relations between our states, the Soviet side will not resort to force to remove our fishermen from the islands."[16]

The Chinese had condemned the Russians for the deteriorating situation on their common perimeter and the Soviets returned the compliment, adding a few extra flourishes, such as that the infractions of the Soviet frontier with the PRC had assumed a "systematic" character and that the estimated number of these incidents already exceeded five thousand. Again, no specific data were furnished so that one had no way of knowing when and where the events alluded to took place and what exactly they entailed—whether they were minor scrapes that in normal conditions would be disregarded but at this point were inflated out of all proportion or something much more serious. Unluckily for the Soviet case, the sole example cited to illustrate Chinese wrongdoing on this score completely missed the target, for genuine disagreement concerning the ownership of these particular islands had evidently persisted for quite a while. Thus, before the territorial issue even surfaced, a press story dealing with various divergences observed in contemporary PRC and Soviet charts of their shared boundary featured the following account:

> Less spectacular is a difference in mapping an area on the border between China and the Soviet Union [as compared with the magnitude of the discrepancies pictured on the Sino-Mongolian arc]. In this instance a

series of low-lying swampy islands about twenty miles long are claimed by both sides at the confluence of the Amur River and the Ussuri River.

Although the islands adjoin the Siberian metropolitan center of Khabarovsk, they appear to be uninhabited. That is probably why the territorial dispute, if one exists in fact, has not gone beyond the mapping stage.[17]

In light of the above, to describe Chinese efforts to establish a physical presence on the contested islands as an infringement of the Soviet frontier, as though the latter's status here was definitively fixed and put the Soviet Union in absolute possession of the islands, showed singular aplomb, although little respect for legal accuracy. Actually, how brazen the Kremlin's bid, how fictitious its claim, and how deceptive the drift of the news report's speculation on whether a territorial dispute even existed or amounted to more than a few paltry cartographical inconsistencies can only be appreciated in retrospect.

THE BORDER RIVER ISSUE: A RETROSPECTIVE NOTE

By the 1970s, a completely different picture of what had been happening at the time was making the rounds. The Chinese, as already mentioned, had revealed that they had occasion to complain to the Soviets as far back as 1959-60 about frequent Soviet incursions into "Chinese-owned" islands in the border rivers. The stories lately circulated by the Soviets, if true, also leave no doubt that these various islands were the site of constant bickering. To cite a recent Soviet account of that experience, the most detailed (and lurid) recital to date of Chinese misdeeds in this precinct:

> Beginning with the summer of 1962, the violations of the Soviet border by the Chinese side became more regular and assumed an acute character. There were a particularly large number of violations of the border along the river banks of the Argun, the Amur and the Ussuri. In 1963 over three thousand cases of Soviet islands being entered by Chinese citizens were recorded, and, together with Chinese infringements of Soviet river frontiers, there were over four thousand incidents of this kind during the year (involving over 100 thousand people).
> The violations of border regulations by the Chinese side were an endeavor to occupy Soviet islands and parts of Soviet territory along the land and river frontiers post factum.

The willful entry of Soviet islands by Chinese citizens, obviously encouraged by their authorities, was accompanied in many cases by hooliganism and outrageous behavior towards Soviet frontier guardsmen. When the offenders were requested to leave Soviet territory they usually refused to do so. Chinese frontier representatives and officials made territorial claims at meetings with representatives of our border authorities.

The Soviet government repeatedly pointed out to the Chinese government that such willful acts violating border regulations were inadmissible and suggested that the question should be settled in a friendly manner. The government of the PRC would invariably justify the actions of its citizens and servicemen who had violated the Soviet-Chinese border.

Several Soviet notes and statements of the USSR embassy in the PRC pointed out that "the existing regulations" on the border were being violated by Chinese citizens and serviceman and that Soviet frontiersmen were guarding the border along the delimited line.[18]

Against such a background, the premier attempt to portray the islands as obviously Soviet property that the Chinese surreptitiously tried to encroach upon strikes one as a rather ingenuous mise en scène, designed to promote the cause of the status quo and disguise the extent and potency of the "revisionist" challenge to the de facto situation.

More pertinent was Moscow's companion disclosure that "the Soviet government has already proposed many times to the government of the People's Republic of China that consultations be held on the question of the demarcation of specific sections of the frontier line, so as to exclude any possibility of misunderstanding," but that, reportedly, "the Chinese side evades such consultations, while at the same time continuing to violate the border." Commented the Soviet note: "This cannot but make us wary, especially in view of the fact that Chinese propaganda is giving clear hints alleging that there has been unjust demarcation of some sections of the Soviet-Chinese border in the past."[19]

In a sense, it is strange that the Soviets had waited so long to play this card. Elementary logic dictated the move. In his initial sally, Khrushchev had singled out negotiations as the proper means for settling the Sino-Indian border conflict. The latest manifesto again emphasized that "Communists consistently work for the solution of frontier problems through negotiation" and trumpeted the message that "the socialist countries, guided in their relations by the principle of proletarian internationalism, should show other peoples an example in the friendly solution of territorial problems." At some juncture, these brave-sounding words had to be converted into suitable deeds in order to forestall loss of credibility. By advertising that the Soviet chiefs had urged their Chinese counterparts to sit down with them and talk these matters over, in vain we are told, Moscow presently sought to persuade its global audience that it lived by the rules it preached and, by the same token, to cast Peking in the role of the official villain. Furthermore, the very slogan of "peaceful methods of resolving international differences" was altogether too valuable a sales pitch to let the Chinese preempt it without a challenge.

Also quite true to Khrushchev's "style" in the current debate was the careful omission of any hint of a basic divergence between the Soviet and PRC conceptions of the agenda for such a conference. Peking had indicated from the outset its desire to see the entire extent of the boundary retraced; Moscow mentioned only the "demarcation of specific sections of the frontier line," totally ignoring known Chinese wishes on that count and then feigning surprise that the leaders of the PRC did not respond with enthusiasm to the "reasonable" Soviet offer. Reasonable it might have been, but it did not fit Peking's plans. And, on the diplomatic scene, advocating a formula that intentionally disregards the other party's point of view is seldom conducive to positive results, unless, of course, the whole purpose of the exercise is to post a propaganda victory and not to strive for a real consensus.

Until now the Soviets had kept busy heaping abuse on their Chinese comrades. They still had not said anything constructive in defense of the existing Sino-Soviet frontier to parry Peking's suggestion that, since that boundary rested on a series of treaties the validity of which, due to their "unequal" nature, was highly dubious, the boundary's own legitimacy was equally impaired. Nevertheless, some kind of rebuttal was needed, and the Kremlin's communique next tackled this difficult job with the plea that

> the artificial creation, in our times, of any territorial problems—especially between socialist countries— would amount to entering on a very dangerous path. If, today, countries begin making territorial claims on one another, using as arguments certain ancient data and the graves of their forefathers, if they start fighting to revise the historically developed frontiers, this will lead to no good, but will merely create feuds among all peoples, to the joy of the enemies of peace.

It should not be forgotten that questions of territorial disputes and claims have often in the past been the source of acute friction and conflict between states, a source inflaming nationalist passions. It is common knowledge that territorial disputes and frontier conflicts have been used as pretexts for wars of conquest. . . .

The Soviet Union has no frontier conflict with any of her neighboring states. And we are proud of this, because this situation is in line not only with the interests of the Soviet Union, but also with the interests of all the socialist countries and the interests of world peace.[20]

The brief was a curious one, both for what it contained and what it left out. First, no attempt was made to summon the authority of international law, although its precepts were certainly relevant to the occasion. The Soviets might have been willing to reproach the Chinese for turning the "ideological dispute" into a state issue, but they were not about to expose themselves to a similar charge and steered clear of "juridifying" the tenor of the dialogue. So, if the Chinese Communists had banked on maneuvering their Soviet allies into flying to the support of the tsarist agreements, they must have been sorely disappointed. Second, the authors of the Soviet document relied on the shopworn contention of every champion of the status quo—in this instance donning the mask of "historically developed frontiers"—against the protagonists of change, to wit, that any such undertaking owed promise of destroying the civilized world. Third, the chosen formula of "historically developed frontiers" was itself both interesting and symptomatic, for it sought to defend the established order by portraying it as a spontaneous outgrowth of some kind of impersonal forces, thereby filling it with a "natural" quality and shielding it from criticism for human failure or responsibility. Fourth, Moscow's spokesmen, quite advisedly, forebore decrying the dangers of "territorial revisionism" within the narrow frame alone of the Sino-Soviet polemics, since a parochial focus was bound to reduce the force of their argument, but, instead, keyed the lecture to general experience and thus, presumably, hoped to universalize the appeal of the Kremlin's case.

We end up with the picture of a Khrushchev administration intent on injecting the "territorial" theme into the mainstream of the mounting Sino-Soviet doctrinal controversy and of exploiting to the full the advantages perceived in publicizing the "cardinal sin" attributed to the PRC leadership of pursuing a policy of "geographical expansionism." For, one must remember, it was Moscow that was pushing the article. Up to this point, the Chinese had contributed little on the subject, and most of it was couched in the tone of a warning and a query—more or less alerting the Soviets to the risk they ran if they insisted on trifling with matches and asking them if they actually had in mind to start a fire. Peking moved to block the opening blow and stopped; Moscow carried the fight a step further.

THE SOVIET PROPAGANDA BATTLE

The previous pattern of rhetoric continued to hold. Inasmuch as the Kremlin was waging a propaganda battle, legal devices did not recommend themselves to it. Conversely, an emotional attack on those who succumbed to the evils of militant nationalism, exhibited warlike tendencies, and manufactured frontier incidents offered a double attraction. In the name of "proletarian internationalism," by whose code both capitals professed to regulate their behavior, the Chinese Communist hierarchy could be pilloried for the crime of "nationalist particularism" and its prestige within the so-called "socialist commonwealth" and the international Communist system effectively undermined as a consequence. In "bourgeois" circles and among nonaligned governments, Peking's influence would also suffer a serious decline if the idea that the PRC regime harbored grandiose plans of conquest and aggression ever took root. That is why the Soviets kept harping on the Sino-Indian border <u>contretemps</u>: to cater to the impression that they were more disturbed by Chinese transgressions in this quarter than any possible peril to themselves.[21] Khrushchev's bid for popular sympathy at home and abroad in his anti-Mao campaign was rather obvious. And the parting shot about the Soviet Union's having any other frontier problems both drew an invidious comparison, for foreign consumption, between its record in this domain and that of the PRC and subtly informed anybody else who aspired to "revise" the topography of the Soviet boundary that the subject was strictly forbidden.

Distortion, willful exaggeration, plain fabrication, assigning to the PRC leaders sinister designs of territorial aggrandizement without a shred of proof to sustain the accusation—all this was pressed into service in order to score in a shrewd game of political one-upmanship contrived to strengthen Moscow's hand within the ranks of the Communist club and enhance its stature on the outer stage, a contest in which the business of the frontiers furnished a welcome means toward extraneous ends and swung little weight on its own. In sum, with the Sino-Soviet doctrinal dispute then rising to a new crescendo, either Khrushchev felt that the territorial issue was too potent a diplomatic weapon not to wield it against his PRC opponents, or, having gone to the trouble of digging up a suitable hobby-horse, he was prepared to ride it for all it was worth.

That the drift of the Soviet communication here amounted to a deliberate exacerbation of the tenor of the Moscow-Peking controversy is undeniable. Yet, the "escalation" was a finely calibrated one and retained a due sense of proportion. In particular, although the Soviets were quick to denounce the Chinese comrades for diverting an ideological discussion into governmental channels and used this as a pretext to turn to the same media, they still stopped short of officially "legalizing" the debate. Besides the many factors already mentioned which conspired against such a move, the Kremlin's decision to emphasize the tenets of "proletarian internationalism" and Peking's alleged violation thereof compounded the difficulties of openly resorting to the language of the law: to make a good legal case for the Soviet Union, a "national" approach was a sine qua non—promoting USSR rights versus PRC rights, USSR claims versus PRC claims, USSR title versus PRC title, and so forth, none of which squared with the "internationalist" thesis that Moscow was propounding. Hence, the law was left untouched, and less confining methods were relied upon in prosecuting the waxing war of words.

CPSU Letter, November 29, 1963

A similar theme recurred in the CPSU Letter of November 29, 1963,[22] where, at one point, the Chinese comrades were told:

> You will probably agree that the situation which has arisen in recent years along different sections of the Soviet-Chinese border cannot be regarded as normal. The Soviet government has already proposed that friendly consultations take place to define accurately the boundary in different sections, considering that this will result in removal of the causes of the present misunderstanding. Recently you, too, spoke in favor of solving this question on the basis of mutual consultation. In this connection, we are transmitting to you a relevant document.
> Statements have recently been made in China concerning the aggressive policy of the tsarist government and the unjust treaties imposed upon China. Naturally, we will not defend the Russian tsars who permitted arbitrariness in laying down the state boundaries with neighboring countries. We are convinced that you, too, do not intend to defend the Chinese emperors who by force of arms seized not a few territories belonging to others. But while condemning the reactionary actions of the top-strata exploiters who held power in Russia and in China

at that time, we cannot disregard the fact that historically-formed boundaries between states now exist. Any attempt to ignore this can become the source of misunderstandings and conflicts; at the same time, they will not lead to the solution of the problem. It would be simply unreasonable to create territorial problems artificially at the present time, when the working class is in power and when our common aim is communism, under which state borders will gradually lose their former significance. We have all the possibilities for fully eliminating border frictions of any kind, and thus showing the peoples an example of truly friendly relations between two socialist states.

While largely repeating the gist of the earlier message, the latest communication did strike one new note. Instead of simply denying in general terms the propriety of resorting to historical evidence to "fabricate" territorial claims, the present statement went a step farther. Without admitting the validity of the Chinese charge concerning "the aggressive policy of the tsarist government and the unjust treaties imposed upon China," the Soviets made a show of recognizing that the tsarist government's record on that score may have been rooted in arbitrariness and disavowing any desire to defend their predecessors' performance in this domain. However, they also immediately exacted a quid pro quo for their concession by faulting past Chinese conduct on identical grounds and voicing the presumption that the current mainland leadership would not wish to champion the merits of the expansionist practices of its dynastic forefathers either.

In sum, from abstract reference to the use of history in support of territorial claims, Moscow shifted to concrete discussion of the Russo-Chinese experience in this context and, in the process, agreed that the Soviet case here was porous if viewed from a historical perspective, but, by the same token, found the PRC position equally shaky. The clear implication is that history was an uncertain counsellor at best when it came to articulating territorial demands and, in the specific circumstances of Russo-Chinese relations, the testimony of the old chronicles in fact availed neither side, for by its standards both were right or both were wrong. At that juncture, the solution had to be determined by other considerations, such as effective possession, self-determination, and so forth, and these criteria tended to work to the Kremlin's advantage. Or, if the PRC nevertheless persisted in dredging up historical memorabilia for "revisionist" purposes, the Soviets, invoking the principle of equivalence, were just as free then to apply the same technique to them and presumably impugn PRC title to vast tracts of land acquired long ago in analogously arbitrary fashion—from the Russians or other adjacent nations.[23]

Khrushchev's Letter, December 21, 1963

A few months later, Khrushchev tried a different tack with the dispatch, on December 21, 1963, of a letter to the governments of all countries that called for the conclusion of a convention renouncing the use of force in the settlement of territorial and frontier disputes.[24] In substantive terms, the circular contained no surprises. The old dichotomy between situations in which, for various reasons, recourse to coercion was licensed as an instrumentality for effecting a change in the operative boundary line and those contingencies where such a solution was a priori barred was spelled out once more, in richer detail this time. Thus, territorial claims "associated with the completion of the liberation of this or that people from colonial oppression or foreign occupation," be it the recovery of a portion of the ancestral soil still under imperialist rule or a struggle of an entire nation for independence, fell into the former category. While, according to the Soviet head of state, the population of the colonies strove to achieve their goal of political emancipation "by peaceful means," these means often proved inadequate because of the resistance of those determined to preserve their ill-gotten gains—by violence if necessary—and so "the oppressed peoples have no choice but to take up arms themselves." Indeed, he declared, "this is their sacred right."

Military bases abroad were likewise not immune from the application of duress to secure their liquidation: though ostensibly sanctioned by treaty clauses, the legality of such installations was nevertheless challenged on grounds that the constitutive pacts were bare <u>diktats</u> that allowed stronger powers to trample on the sovereignty and physical integrity of the weaker host countries. Therefore, whenever the latter insisted that "the treaties on military bases be dissolved, that those territories be restored to them, and that the bases be dismantled and the foreign troops withdrawn," then, in the words of the text, "these just demands should be satisfied." If not, compulsion was presumably in order to attain this objective.

Not subject to the above dispensation were the issues stemming from the partition of several countries in the wake of World War II and since. The matter of reunification of these divided lands was also identified "to a certain extent with the territorial question." The Kremlin urged that the desire of the local inhabitants to form a single state be "treated. . .with understanding and respect," provided the problem was "settled by the peoples of these countries and their governments themselves, without any interference or pressure from the outside and, of course, without foreign military intervention. . . ." But, the message cautioned, "no force should be used in settling this question and the peoples of these countries should be given the opportunity to solve the problems of unification by peaceful means," adding that "all other states should contribute to this."[25]

By Khrushchev's own admission, however, his proposal was primarily focused on another matter, namely, on "how to deal with territorial disputes and claims which arise over the actually existing and well-established frontiers of states." The Soviet note first pinpointed a "special class among such claims" consisting, in its phraseology, of the "demands of the revenge-seeking circles of certain states which were the aggressors in the Second World War, . . . are harboring plans for a revision of the just postwar territorial settlement. . . [and] want to get hold of those territories which went to other states by way of eliminating the consequences of aggression and providing guarantees of security for the future." These "claims," the Kremlin maintained, "must be absolutely rejected, as being incompatible with the interests of peace, because nothing but a new world war can grow out of those claims." As for the rest, which, it conceded, perhaps numbered a majority of the current conflicts generated by rival efforts to assert title to the same piece of territory, plainly enough these "had nothing to do with postwar settlements," and here the parties "put forward arguments and considerations relating to history, ethnography, blood affinity, religion and so on."[26]

In its Statement of September 21, 1963, the Soviet government had already expressed doubts concerning the wisdom of nations seeking to rely on "ancient data and the graves of their forefathers" in pressing for the revision of "historically developed frontiers"; such an attitude merely created deadly feuds between members of the global community. Khrushchev's missive again queried the validity of that procedure, except that on this occasion criticism of the practice was formulated in much more elaborate, comprehensive, and sophisticated fashion. To wit:

> It often happens that one state justifies its territorial claim on another state by such arguments, and the second state in its turn finds other arguments from the same sphere, but of an absolutely opposite nature, and itself puts forward a territorial counterclaim. The result is the fomenting of passions and the deepening of mutual strife.
>
> How can one tell which side is right, whose position is just and whose unjust? In some cases this is very difficult, because the existing frontiers came into being as a result of the influence of many factors.
>
> In many cases, references to history are of no assistance. Who can affirm, say, that a reference to the seventeenth century which one state puts forward in substantia-

tion of its territorial claim, is more valid than, for
instance, a reference to the eighteenth or nineteenth
century by which the other state tries to bolster its own
counterclaim?

And if one were to take as the basis for the solution of
a frontier dispute the whole of history spread over several
millenia, all would agree, one would think, that in many
cases no real solution could be found. Nor can we forget
the fact that not infrequently references to history are
made in order to provide a cover for open aggression, as
was the case, for instance, with Mussolini's references
to the frontiers of the Roman Empire in order to substantiate his seizures of territory in the Mediterranean, which
the Italian fascists even christened "mare nostrum," that
is, "our sea," in an effort to present themselves as the
heirs of the ancient Romans.

Sometimes it is difficult to get one's bearings among the
numerous "arguments" based on national or ethnographic
grounds, or grounds of blood affinity. The development
of mankind has been such that some peoples are now
living on the territories of a number of states. On the
other hand, there exist states of a multinational type,
sometimes inhabited by dozens of peoples, even belonging
to different races.

Unfortunately, disputes about frontiers take place not
only between historians and ethnographers, but also between states, each of which possesses armed forces, and
sometimes quite large ones. Life itself shows that the
majority of territorial disputes are fraught with the danger of relations between the parties becoming complicated,
with the possibility of a serious armed conflict, and consequently constitute a potential threat to universal peace.
This means that due understanding of frontiers, as they
have been formed in the course of history, has to be
displayed.[27]

In short, for Khrushchev, the weakness of a tradition-oriented
approach to territorial rights lay in that the data culled from anti-
quated records could easily be cited both pro and con by either side
in a squabble over ownership of some slice of terrain, that the facts
so adduced failed to demonstrate the superiority of one advocate's
contentions over his competitor's, that the norm itself was largely
obsolete and ran counter to modern social conditions which had
transcended the constricting limits of a purely ethnic concept of
human organization, and that recourse to evidence of this genre

STALEMATE

only sowed the seeds of international discord. All this counselled reserve in invoking the testimony of the past as a rationale for altering the realities of the present, but the Soviet document was also very careful not to convey the impression of a total repudiation by the Soviet Union of the value of "historical rights" per se: the annals of Soviet diplomacy are replete with examples of resort to historical arguments to vindicate Moscow's actions, and the prospective usefulness of history as an alibi under similar circumstances loomed far too great to discard so handy a tool just yet.

To the Soviets, the worst danger from military outbreaks over frontiers centered on Europe. Elsewhere as well, though, the price of wars to decide possession of a contested area was deemed to be prohibitive and not to warrant these extreme measures. Not unexpectedly, then, the letter concluded that

> there are not, nor can there be, territorial disputes in out time between states already formed, or unresolved frontier questions, of such a kind that it is permissible to use armed force in order to settle them. No, this cannot be allowed to happen, and we must do everything possible to rule out the possibility of events developing in such a way.[28]

The note did acknowledge the occurrence of genuine frontier problems that required concerted attention. Without purporting to ignore these, it simply registered anew its opposition to any "military methods of settling territorial disputes," appealed for a thorough exploration of all peaceful avenues apt to produce a consensus and assured its mass audience, rather truistically, that "life itself shows that whenever states firmly abide by the principles of peaceful coexistence and display good will, restraint and due regard for each other's interests, they are quite capable of extricating themselves from the maze of historical, national, geographic, and other factors and finding a satisfactory solution."[29] Mentioned as effective devices in that connection were direct negotiations between the states involved, the use of good offices, requests for assistance from international organizations, the machinery of the United Nations, and so on.

Accordingly, the Soviet government called for the signature of a universal convention that would "include the following principal propositions":

1. A solemn undertaking by the states, parties to the agreement, not to resort to force to alter the existing state frontiers;

2. Recognition that the territory of states should not, even temporarily, be the object of any invasion, attack, military occupa-

tion or any other forcible measures directly or indirectly undertaken by other states for whatsoever political, economic, strategic, frontier, or any other considerations;

3. A firm declaration that neither differences in social or political systems, nor denial of recognition or the absence of diplomatic relations, nor any other pretexts can serve as justification for the violation by any one state of the territorial integrity of another;

4. An undertaking to settle all territorial disputes exclusively by peaceful means, such as negotiations, mediation, conciliatory procedure, and also other peaceful means at the choice of the parties concerned in conformity with the United Nations Charter.

A postscript read: "Needless to say, such an international agreement should cover all territorial disputes concerning the existing frontiers between states."[30]

It is not our purpose here to analyze in depth the jural caliber of Khrushchev's message. The exercise would accomplish little in any case, for the chief criticism that can be levelled at its contents was the bland, unimaginative, and stock quality of its prescriptions.[31] Moreover, an elaborate assessment of the legal merits of the project would in this instance be quite irrelevant since this study focuses on the dynamics of the Sino-Soviet controversy and, as will be shown, the Chinese did not bother to comment *ad rem* on the various elements of the plan advanced ty Khrushchev and brushed the idea aside after a minimal attempt to deal with just one dimension of the blueprint in semisubstantive fashion. The sole purpose of summing up the highlights of Khrushchev's prospectus, then, was that a survey might indicate what it was that the document featured or omitted that precipitated or colored Peking's brusque refusal to endorse its dicta.

PRC REACTION TO SOVIET BID

Indeed, the only official explanation volunteered by the PRC regime for its negative response to the Soviet bid, articulated in Chou En-lai's report on the results of his visit to 14 lands,[32] was that

> this proposal deliberately confused imperialist aggression and occupation of other countries' territories with territorial disputes and boundary questions between nations left over by history. Of course, boundary questions between Asian and African countries should and could find a fair and reasonable solution through peaceful consultations. This was also the case with boundary questions

between socialist countries. But imperialist aggression
and occupation of other countries' territories was a
matter of a completely different nature. As to countries
whose territories had been invaded and occupied by
imperialism, they naturally had every right to recover
their lost territories by any means. To ask those
countries which were subjected to aggression to renounce the use of force in any circumstances was in fact
to ask the people of all countries to renounce their
struggle against the imperialist policies of aggression
and war, placing themselves at the mercy of imperialism
and submitting to imperialist enslavement.[33]

From the above passage, the Chinese seemed to take exception
to two particular aspects of Moscow's draft formula. First, by
inference, they appeared to want to exclude the frontiers between
non-Asian, non-African, and nonsocialist countries from the workings
of the veto against the employment of coercion to amend their present
configuration. Second, they argued in favor of a further differentiation
between interstate boundary lines born of true historical accident and
presumably neutral in a political sense and those tainted with an imperialist association. Khrushchev had drawn a distinction only between
the unfinished business of emancipation from colonial rule, in which
recourse to compulsion to achieve a final solution was acceptable,
and disagreements over the placement of current boundaries in the
affairs of recognized, equally sovereign states, where such conduct
was barred.

By contrast, the Chinese Communists implied that in the latter
category, too, the functioning frontiers were not prima facie immune
from violent change if imperialism had played a role in determining
their complexion and if imperialistic motives still operated to prevent
the consummation of an appropriate readjustment in the territorial
status quo by pacific means. To illustrate the discrepancy in concrete terms: under the Soviet concept, the Sino-Indian frontier quarrel
automatically fitted the bill of a "dispute opposing established states"
in which due attention would have to be paid to today's "historically
defined boundaries"; in the PRC version, if these boundaries were
the product of imperialist expansionism and imperialistic appetites
stood behind the efforts to maintain them intact, they were not, on
those grounds alone, exempt from suitable revision by dint of exertion
of physical pressure, if need be. Much the same can be said, of
course, of the origins of the Sino-Russian border, save that the
principle of proletarian internationalism theoretically supervened to
preclude use of force between "fraternal nations"—pursuant to the
PRC thesis, an eventual accommodation was imperative here as

well, but meantime duress ought not to be applied to accomplish the goal.

No statute of limitations shielded the estate of the "offender" and, on the whole, the PRC statement sounded as though Peking was prepared to countenance resort to arms vis-a-vis a wider class of border phenomena than the Kremlin, at least judging from the letter of their respective public pronouncements. Generally, in a verbal pattern that had become typical of the Sino-Soviet dialogue, the PRC leaders set a higher value on violence as a tool to "combat imperialism" and attributed greater danger to the "machinations of the imperialist camp" on the contemporary scene than did their Soviet colleagues. Khrushchev's offer thus also fell victim to the ongoing controversy over the correctness of the policy emphasizing peaceful coexistence as compared with a program extolling the virtues of revolutionary militancy.

These are minor points, however, and can hardly account for the vehemence of the Chinese reaction. On most essentials, the document fulfilled the accepted doctrinal criteria. The customary carte blanche was granted the so-called national liberation movements in their drive to shed the few remaining vestiges of former dependency, Chinese contentions to the contrary notwithstanding. All the standard ideological nuances were scrupulously observed, and friend and foe were filed under familiar rubrics. The text likewise avoided any hint of anti-Chinese static. The sole reference to the People's Republic of China unconditionally affirmed the PRC's right to "free" Taiwan by whatever process it pleased; and, in apparent deference to Peking's susceptibilities, the examples of neither Hong Kong nor Macao were presently adduced as comparable experiences.[34] For once, the Soviets even abstained from voicing disparaging remarks about the Sino-Indian border imbroglio, which is quite understandable: if Khrushchev wished to reap maximum support for his initiative, the last thing in the world he could afford to do was put the nonaligned nations in the position of having to commit themselves on such an explosive issue.[35]

AN ANALYSIS OF THE SOVIET COMMUNICATION

The material contents of the Soviet communication, then, were not calculated to provoke Peking's anger. Yet, the episode certainly did, which suggests that a closer look at the formal aspects of the incident may be in order. Viewed from that angle, Peking's irritation begins to make more sense. The thrust and timing of the Moscow message, for instance, clearly aimed to exploit the emotions aroused by the Himalayan confrontation and, by implication, to condemn the

STALEMATE   89

brand of behavior that on this occasion had culminated in bloodletting.[36]
Hence, despite the oblique phrasing, no doubt can be entertained that
the People's Republic of China, because of its role in that affair, was
among the principal targets, if not the principal one, of the Soviet
stratagem. Further, Khrushchev's proposal was greeted primarily as
a legal venture and in home circles was discussed chiefly in that
vein,[37] whereas international law was not a Chinese Communist forte
and the blatant appeal to its norms by supposed confederates did not,
one is morally convinced, sit well with the men running the PRC.

Add to that the fact that the gesture was addressed to every
nation on the globe without discriminating between class kin and enemy
and envisaged that relations between all of them, whether they be
members of the inner sanctum, or neutrals, or sworn antagonists,
be governed by the same code, and it is easy to see why the Chinese
should have felt betrayed. To the Peking authorities, the very thought
of signing a key political treaty in the company of the pillars of the
Western community was anathema at that stage. The Soviets must
have known it and nonetheless tried to maneuver the Chinese into a
corner where they either would have to act against what they frankly
professed to believe in or reject the bid and so isolate themselves
from the mainstream of world opinion. Not the least of Khrushchev's
expectations must have been that the Chinese would choose precisely
the latter course and enable him to capitalize at will on the widespread
anti-Chinese sentiment such a decision would infallibly foster.

Finally, while there was no reason to assume that the Sino-
Soviet debate over the territorial issue would ever turn into a serious
problem, still, with the sharpened awareness that at some juncture
it might conceivably come to a practical test, the knowledge that
public sympathies were solidly arrayed against the use of force to
redress an alleged wrong in initially fixing the boundary line was
bound to give comfort to the Soviets and, by the same token, work to
handicap their PRC rivals. The appreciation that, propaganda-wise,
the Soviets, perhaps in anticipation of that very contingency, had
neatly stacked the deck in their own favor, could not but gall the
PRC comrades. What is more, the prospect that in the event a border
crisis between the Soviet Union and the People's Republic of China were
to erupt, every government on earth would be dragged into the family
squabble or could horn in by claiming a valid interest derived from a
universal convention of the kind advocated by Khrushchev, again was
not prone to mollify the PRC leaders.

The net impression is that of a successful publicity stunt staged
by the Kremlin. Not a shred of evidence can be found to show that
the Soviets launched the experiment in genuine fear of an imminent
Chinese threat to the Soviet Union's territorial integrity or even as a
safeguard against the remote possibility of such a situation developing

in the near future. Indeed, the subsequent fate of the project whose unveiling evoked so much fanfare and which, within a twelve-month period, ended up consigned to oblivion, proves that it was little else than an expendable pawn in a collateral chess game spun out for the sake of salesmanship alone and with the design to enhance one's image and build up one's credit and undercut the competitor's.

The core theme did not vary. The only novelty was the overt introduction of international law terminology: the audience was different. As long as the conversation stayed "private," both parties could avoid "juridifying" the exchange; once the polemics had been transferred to open chambers, the topic was general, and employing international law arguments couched at the highest level of abstraction did not then serve to "legalize" the purely Sino-Soviet share of the affair. The scenery was slightly modified, but the lyrics of the central duet were unaffected by the shift.

NOTES

1. Pravda, Mar. 30, 1969; Izvestiya, Mar. 30, 1969, pp. 1-2; USSR Government Statement of March 29, 1969, Moscow, 1969, p. 12.
2. A. Kruchinin, V. Olgin, Territorial Claims of Mao Tse-tung: History and Modern Times, Moscow, n.d., p. 94.
3. Statement of the Government of the People's Republic of China, May 24, 1969, China Reconstructs, 1969, No. 7, Suppl., p. 6 (hereafter abbr. as CR).
4. Down with the New Tsars! Soviet Revisionists' Anti-China Atrocities on the Heilung and Wusuli Rivers, Peking, 1969, n.d.
5. Cf., A. Kruchinin, V. Olgin, op. cit., p. 94: "But the Chinese leadership continued to make trouble on the border. Then, seeing that the illegal activities on the border did not yield the desired results and realizing that it would not be in their interests to continue ignoring the Soviet proposal, the Chinese side was compelled to agree to the holding of the consultations." The Chinese, on the other hand, simply say that their "reasonable proposal" of Aug. 23, 1963, "was brazenly rejected by the Soviet side." Down with the New Tsars!
6. This is especially true when one bears in mind that some Soviet authors now emphasize that although by virtue of the Treaty of Nerchinsk "formally the Tsing Empire was given the right to the territories outlined by the Treaty. . . it didn't exercise full sovereignty there because of the Manchu representatives' oath, which they followed, not to erect buildings in the place of former Russian ostrogs (blockhouses)," and cite this evidence to support the inference that these lands were never fully acquired by the Middle Kingdom and the

STALEMATE   91

latter's title to them remained inchoate. For example, V. S. Myasnikov, "Russian-Chinese Relations in the Seventeenth Century (documents and materials)," (dittoed), p. 12.

7. The Origin and Development of the Differences between the Leadership of the CPSU and Ourselves, Peking, 1963; Peking Review, 1963, No. 37, pp. 6-23 (hereafter abbr. as PR). The July 14 Open Letter from the CPSU did not refer to the frontier controversy.

8. The Origin and Development, p. 32.

9. Ibid., p. 47. In the Western press, the Chinese remarks about "Soviet large-scale subversive activities in the Ili region" were in some instances pictured as a charge that the Russians "had attempted to overthrow the Chinese local government at Ili." See Asian Recorder, 1963, p. 5459. In the absence of other information, the correctness of this interpretation is open to doubt. That the Soviets fomented trouble in the Ili area may be taken for granted; that they went so far as to plot the overthrow of the local government is not clear even from the data furnished by Chinese sources.

10. Cf., New York Times, Feb. 21, 1967, p. 12: "The Soviet consulates in Sinkiang played a major role in helping to stir up this [1962] trouble, according to Russian emigres then living in the area. Clandestine Russian political and subversive activity among the non-Chinese minorities is believed by many informed sources to have continued."

11. No specific allegations concerning differences of opinion over the profile of the USSR-PRC frontier in the Sinkiang region were aired at this time. The Russians were accused of political meddling in Sinkiang's internal affairs. This interference and the turmoil in the area did, however, occasion collisions on the frontier stemming apparently from Chinese attempts to interdict the flight of refugees into the USSR and Soviet countermeasures against Chinese pursuit of the fugitives into Soviet territory.

12. See, for instance, A. Ya. Kryazhev, "Izvrashchenie maoistami leninskoi natsionalnoi politiki," Izvestiya Sibirskogo Otdeleniya Akademii Nauk SSSR, seriya obshchestvennykh nauk, 1976, No. 1, vyp. 1, p. 104, where the author adds that a mass of refugees streamed from Sinkiang toward the Soviet Union, Afghanistan, Turkey, Saudi Arabia, and other countries, numbering more than 200,000 individuals by 1974. Cf., New York Times, Feb. 21, 1967, p. 8: "Refugee reports in Hongknog as well as hints in both the Chinese and Soviet press tend to confirm that in 1962 bloody and large-scale Chinese shooting of Turkic peoples took place after anti-Chinese demonstrations in Sinkiang."

13. O. Borisov, B. Koloskov, "Politika Sovetskogo Soyuza v otnoshenii KNR—sotsialisticheskii internatsionalizm v deistvii (sovetsko-kitaiskie otnosheniya v 1948-1967gg)," in Leninskaya

politika SSSR v otnoshenii Kitaya, Moscow, 1968, pp. 208-10; O. B. Borisov, B. T. Koloskov, Sovetsko-Kitaiskie otnosheniya 1945-1970, kratkii ocherk, Moscow, 1971, pp. 274-77; Vneshnyaya politika i mezhdunarodnye otnosheniya Kitaiskoi Narodnoi Respubliki 1959-1963, Moscow, 1974, Vol. 1, pp. 239-40 (it is interesting to note that this last source [p. 232] claims that in 1960 the PRC refused to sign an agreement concerning citizenship and the legal protection of citizens of both countries); S. G. Yurkov, Pekin: Novaya politika?, Moscow, 1972, p. 60; M. S. Kapitsa, Levee zdravogo smysla (O vnesh-nei politike gruppy Mao), Moscow, 1968, pp. 70-71; idem, KNR: dva desyatiletiya-dve politiki, Moscow, 1969, pp. 195-97.

Figures on the number of people who fled from Sinkiang to Soviet territory differ. Thus, Asian Recorder, 1963, p. 5459, reports that about 50,000 souls fled across the border into Soviet Central Asia since the fall of 1962 (estimated as of October 1963). The same statistics are quoted in Facts on File, Sept. 12-18, p. 324, which attributed the exodus to "hunger and religious persecution."

14. A Reply to Peking (Soviet Booklet No. 122), London, 1963, p. 3. For the complete text of the Soviet Government statement of Sept. 21, 1963, see Pravda, Sept. 21-22, 1963; Vneshnyaya politika Sovetskogo Soyuza i mezhdunarodnye otnosheniya, sbornik dokumentov, 1963 god, Moscow, 1964, pp. 236-87; Soviet News, 1963, No. 4896, pp. 159-64, and No. 4897, pp. 167-74; Moscow News, special issue, Sept. 24, 1963.

15. A Reply to Peking, p. 23. Also, New Times, 1963, No. 39, p. 44.

16. A Reply to Peking, p. 24. To the same effect, see the front page editorial in Pravda, Sept. 23, 1963.

17. New York Times, Feb. 26, 1961, p. 20. The news item adds that: "Not even scholarly Soviet studies refer to the Amur island discrepancy. For example, a historical review of the formation of the Soviet-Chinese Amur River frontier, reviewed in the July, 1960, issue of Voprosy istorii, a Soviet historical journal, discussed the history of the frontier in considerable detail but ignored the map differences." The review in question by G. P. Basharin, published in Voprosy istorii, 1960, No. 7, pp. 160-62, is of the book by P. I. Kabanov, Amurskii vopros, Blagoveshchensk, 1959.

18. A. Kruchinin, V. Olgin, op. cit., pp. 93-94. Also, O. B. Borisov, B. T. Koloskov, op. cit., p. 302.

19. A Reply to Peking, p. 24; Soviet News, 1963, No. 4987, p. 170.

20. A Reply to Peking, pp. 24-25. Refer to the statement which appeared in the editorial entitled "Dangerous Seat of Tension in Asia," Pravda, Sept. 19, 1963, reprinted in Soviet News, 1963, No. 4895, pp. 157-58, and No. 4896, p. 165: "As to the Soviet Union,

STALEMATE 93

it treats with respect the countries bordering on it. It understands that good neighborliness is possible only if the frontiers existing between states are respected."

21. A vivid illustration of this technique is the long essay cited in the previous footnote devoted entirely to the "disastrous consequences of the Chinese-Indian border conflict for the cause of peace." See Soviet News, 1963, No. 4895, p. 157.

22. See W. E. Griffith, Sino-Soviet Relations, 1964-1965, Cambridge, Mass., and London, MIT Press, 1966, p. 151.

23. Subsequently, this is exactly what the Soviets did proceed to do. By branding the Treaty of Nerchinsk a product of wanton Manchu aggression against peaceful Russian settlements in the Amur River basin and thus itself an unequal treaty, Russian spokesmen have laid the ground for a claim for the return of the lands south of the Amur River from which the Russians were unlawfully ousted by a dictated treaty backed by resort to superior armed force. Official Soviet sources have since also emphasized that the Chinese possession of Sinkiang and Inner Mongolia, for instance, was based on military conquest and large-scale destruction of the native population.

24. Pravda, Jan. 4, 1964; Vneshnyaya politika Sovetskogo Soyuza, pp. 343-57; A Call for a Treaty Renouncing the Use of Force in the Settlement of Territorial and Frontier Disputes (Soviet Booklet, Vol. 2, No. 2), London, 1964; Soviet News, 1964, No. 4938, pp. 5-8.

25. A Call for a Treaty, pp. 6-8.
26. Ibid., p. 9.
27. Ibid., pp. 9-10.
28. Ibid., pp. 13-14.
29. Ibid., p. 14.
30. Ibid., pp. 16, 18. The formalities were left to be worked out later and Khrushchev sounded as though this aspect of the problem would prove relatively simple: "As for the forms of a future international agreement on the renunciation by states of the use of force for settling territorial disputes, and also the procedure for conducting talks on the conclusion of this agreement, it seems to me that it would not be very difficult to reach agreement on this, if, of course, the sides concerned show an interest in it. The Soviet government, for its part, is ready to do everything possible to facilitate the solution of these questions."

31. Cf., F. Monconduit, "La Note Khrouchtchev du 31 décembre 1963 relative au réglement pacifique des litiges territoriaux," Annuaire français de droit international, 1964, Paris, 1964, pp. 62-63.

32. PR, 1964, No. 18, pp. 6-12.
33. Ibid., p. 12.
34. However, both are mentioned by P. Smolenskii, Diplomatiya i granitsy, Moscow, 1965, pp. 37-38. This brochure, though, went to

print in March 1965 and was written at a time when Soviet official circles had dropped their conciliatory tone and stepped up their denunciation of the Peking regime as a result of the remarks made by Mao in his talk with a group of Japanese socialists.

With the subsequent deterioration of Sino-Soviet relations, Soviet secondary sources lost their inhibition against mentioning Hong Kong and Macao and discussing Chinese failure to liberate these two colonial vestiges. Such references are now common in the pertinent Soviet literature. See, for example, B. Zanegin, Nationalist Background of China's Foreign Policy, Moscow, n.d., pp. 44-45, 47; I. Gavrilov, Duplicity (on double-dealing policy of Peking splitters), Moscow, n.d., pp. 35-40.

35. References to the Sino-Indian border conflict nevertheless appeared in the contemporary Russian literature devoted to an analysis of the legal significance of Khrushchev's circular letter. See, for instance, P. Smolenskii, op. cit., p. 48; S. Molodtsov, Peace to Frontiers!, Moscow, 1965, p. 9; B. M. Klimenko, Gosudarstvennye granitsy-problema mira, Moscow, 1964, p. 86; K. Ivanov, "National Liberation and Territorial Conflicts," International Affairs, 1964, No. 5, p. 12; V. A. Zorin, V. L. Israelyan, "Marksistsko-leninskii podkhod k resheniyu territorialnykh sporov," Kommunist, 1964, No. 2, p. 30.

36. Invariably, the less specific the reference, the more damning the judgment. Viz., S. Molodtsov, "Frontiers and International Law," International Affairs, 1964, No. 4, p. 11: "There have been instances in recent years of attempts to justify armed attacks undertaken with a view to altering existing boundaries by claims that they did not infringe upon the territorial integrity of the country attacked. The attack, it was claimed in such cases, was made to regain 'our own territory' and rectify incorrectly demarcated borders." To the same effect, G. Tunkin, "Mezhdunarodnoe pravo i gosudarstvennye granitsy," Izvestiya, Jan. 8, 1964. "However, the modern history of international relations knows not a few cases when certain states, attempting to alter by force the existing frontiers, claimed...that their forcible actions did not infringe upon the territory of the other state and that they were merely defending their territory and the frontier, well, ran incorrectly."

37. In addition to the items listed in the three previous footnotes, see I. Blishchenko, "Mezhdunarodnoe pravo i miroe razreshenie sporov," Novoe Vremya, 1964, No. 7, pp. 9-11; B. Dmitriev, "Granitsy gosudarstv i uprochenie mira," Mirovaya ekonomika i mezhdunarodnye otnosheniya, 1964, No. 3, pp. 17-26; G. P. Zador-ozhnyi, Granitsam-mir!, Moscow, 1964; F. Kozhevnikov, A. Piradov, "Mezhdunarodnoe pravo i vopros o granitsakh," Kommunist, 1964, No. 2, pp. 32-38.

4

THE 1964 CONFERENCE

By the end of 1963, the parties probably realized that the rhetorical fusillade had reached a stalemate. The dispute had run as far as it could go without bringing up fresh artillery. All that could be said had been said, and either the original self-imposed limits of the controversy would have to be transcended—and, for the moment at least, the contestants seemed to have no taste for that idea—or a way had to be devised to break the present impasse where each side was determined not to appear to make any concessions to the adversary.

The next report from this sector then indicated that Moscow and Peking had agreed to hold negotiations on the subject of the Sino-Soviet boundary[1] and, on February 23, 1964, "a delegation of Soviet experts on frontier questions" was reported to have "arrived in Peking to discuss certain matters of common interest." The news story, dated February 27, added that already "they have had one meeting with Chinese representatives at which questions of procedure were discussed."[2]

PRELIMINARY SKIRMISHES

To carry on with the current debate would have led nowhere. The move to the bargaining table offered a logical answer. The two capitals had repeatedly advertised their conviction that the problem should properly be handled through bilateral negotiations—the latest step would prove them both right. No prior arrangements had apparently been set concerning the agenda of the session. Indeed, according to a Soviet source, when in its note of November 19, 1963, the PRC government at last signaled its consent to take part in a meeting to consider the border problem, it emphasized that throughout the entire length of the Sino-Soviet frontier there were "many questions requiring discussion" (which the Soviets, in retrospect, saw as an ominous sign) and declined the Soviet offer to publish in the press a joint announcement of the forthcoming conference, pleading "difficulties of agreeing on the text."[3] In a sense, of course, skipping the preliminary technicalities facilitated the meeting, for had the opponents had to define their positions prior to the conference, it might never have convened.[4] Yet, the reverse danger was equally great: having failed to establish the order of business, the Soviet and PRC emissaries, once they began exploring each other's views in earnest, might soon discover that they had no uniform frame of reference and therefore were left with no room for a compromise solution.

This, in fact, is what happened. Soviet and PRC representatives "engaged in consultations in Peking on how best to negotiate border questions between the two countries." A contemporary news item captured the ambiance of the occasion and delivered a singularly prophetic judgment on the prospects for the success of the conversations then in progress:

> According to diplomatic sources, the consultations are being conducted at the embassy level and are aimed at determining whether the Russians and Chinese can find common ground for a discussion of the border issues. The ideological dispute between them has grown worse recently and there is substantial doubt here [in Moscow] whether they will be able to agree on a formula for negotiations.
>
> Moreover, the Chinese Communists are understood to demand that the frontier negotiations be regarded as a comprehensive review of frontier disputes. Such an approach may be interpreted as allowing a reexamination of what the Chinese call "unequal" treaties under which tsarist Russia obtained large areas of Chinese territory.
>
> Soviet officials are said to insist on a more narrow formula under which the negotiations would be limited to minor boundary "adjustments."
>
> This approach would restrict the talks to such problems as the ownership of islands in the Amur and Ussuri Rivers, which form a large segment of the boundary in these streams, and similar local issues.
>
> The best-known issue is a large, almost uninhabited island situated near the Far Eastern city of Khabarovsk, at the junction of the Ussuri and Amur Rivers.[5]

The Soviets clung to their version until the end. On the very eve of the conclave, in his report to a plenary convocation of the Central Committee of the CPSU, Mikhail A. Suslov both criticized the Chinese for their share in precipitating the military confrontation on the Sino-Indian border[6] and repeated the Kremlin's old story about what had meanwhile transpired on the Sino-Soviet frontier. He said:

> We also consider it necessary to tell the plenary meeting about the violations of the Soviet-Chinese border, occasioned through the fault of the Chinese side. This has already been mentioned in the documents of the CPSU and the Soviet government. In 1962 and 1963 violations of the Soviet frontier kept occurring continuously, often assuming the form of crude provocations.
>
> The Soviet government has taken the initiative in proposing that consultations be held in order to specify the frontier line between the Soviet Union and China at certain points. We do so in the belief that no territorial issues exist between the Soviet Union and the People's Republic of China, that the Soviet-Chinese frontier took shape historically, and that the issue can concern only certain sections of the frontier to make them more precise whenever necessary.[7]

And when, in early March, I. V. Spiridonov, head of a Soviet parliamentary delegation visiting India, revealed to the papers in Delhi that a Sino-Soviet mixed commission had been organized, he still described its function solely in terms of demarcation of the border between the Soviet Union and the PRC "in certain sectors." Asked to explain the principles by which the commission would be guided in its task of demarcating the border, he replied that it was possible that some of the border posts had gotten lost or some other similar developments had taken place.[8] Given this evidence, the conclusion is inescapable that the gap between the Soviet and PRC interpretations of the job in store could scarcely be wider.

From what little information is available, it sounds as though efforts to draft a mutually agreeable modus operandi eventually foundered on this key point. Much later, in connection with a piece of serious trouble in the mixed Soviet-Chinese commission on shipping in border sectors of the rivers of the Amur basin—the Soviets accusing the Chinese of deliberately disrupting the work of its fourteenth session which met in Harbin on July 11, 1967—a few stray bits of additional data on what had befallen the border agency bobbed to the surface. First, the Soviets protested, "the Chinese side came out with a number of provocative statements and tried to make the Soviet delegation deal with questions of where the border line should pass—a matter not within the competence of the commission [on border shipping]." Discussion of that subject, the Soviet Foreign Ministry's note next recalled, had been instigated in 1964 between government delegations of the two countries "but was not completed through the fault of the Chinese side" which, we learn,

> had not yet named a date acceptable to it to continue consultations on a more precise demarcation of the Soviet-Chinese border, although the Soviet side, in its proposal of September 28, 1964, expressed its readiness to continue consultations with the Chinese side in Moscow on October 15, 1964.[9]

THE 1964 AFFAIR: THE CHINESE SIDE

Of course, thanks to the wave of revelations triggered by the spate of bloody incidents in 1969 along the Sino-Soviet frontier, a more complete picture of the 1964 affair has since emerged. While refinements attributable to the wisdom of hindsight pose a constant danger, with due caution one can nevertheless mount a fairly accurate reconstruction of the highlights of the encounter. According to Peking's recollections,

> in 1964, the Chinese Government held boundary negotiations with the Soviet Government, during which the Chinese side made it clear that the "Sino-Russian Treaty of Aigun," the "Sino-Russian treaty of Peking" and other treaties relating to the present Sino-Soviet boundary are all unequal treaties tsarist Russian imperialism imposed on China when power was not in the hands of the peoples of China and Russia. But, prompted by the desire to strengthen the revolutionary friendship between the Chinese and Soviet peoples, the Chinese side was willing to take these treaties as the basis for determining the entire alignment of the boundary line between the two countries and for settling all existing questions relating to the boundary; any side which occupies the territory of the other side in violation of the treaties must, in principle, return it wholly and unconditionally to the other side, but this does not preclude necessary readjustments at individual places on the boundary by both sides on the basis of the treaties and in accordance with the principles of consultation on an equal footing and of mutual understanding and mutual accommodation. However, the Soviet side refused to accept the above-mentioned reasonable proposals of the Chinese side. It refused to recognize the treaties relating to the present Sino-Soviet boundary as unequal treaties and obstinately

THE 1964 CONFERENCE

refused to take these treaties as the basis for settling the boundary question between the two countries in its vain attempt to force China to accept a new unequal treaty and thus to perpetuate in legal form its occupation of the Chinese territory which it seized by crossing the boundary line defined by the unequal treaties. This great-power chauvinist and territorial expansionist stand of the Soviet revisionist renegade clique was severely condemned by the Chinese side. The Chinese side clearly pointed out that if the Soviet side should obdurately insist on such a stand and inexorably refuse to mend its ways, the Chinese side will have to reconsider its position as regards the Sino-Soviet boundary question as a whole.[10]

The account duly confirms what was then suspected concerning Peking's rigid insistence on the proximate redefinition of the full extent of the Sino-Soviet boundary line. However, it also sheds light on the gist of the Chinese position at the talks, the details of which the outer world had not known. For instance, if the above statement is correct, this was the first time in the history of the two-year-old debate on the territorial issue that the Chinese formally engaged themselves vis-a-vis the Soviets to observe the core formula by virtue of which tsarist Russia's treaties with imperial China establishing their common frontier would still be accepted, despite their "unequal" character, as "the basis for determining the entire alignment of the boundary line between the two countries and for settling all existing questions relating to the boundary." The Soviet delegation might otherwise have welcomed that particular assurance, except that it came coupled with a sine qua non demand for prior official recognition of the "unequal" nature of the operative border agreements and a blanket commitment to replace the latter with an instrument fixing the whole length of the frontier.

Rather unexpected, too, was the official disclosure corroborating that the Chinese had already at that early date broached the subject of so-called territorial encroachments beyond the confines set by the corresponding conventions: presumably, the river islands, albeit not explicitly identified yet as a major topic of controversy, fell into this special category. The proposed manner of handling this second item of business again fit the usual pattern favored by the Communist Chinese regime: a preliminary acknowledgment that the PRC held original title to the land at stake in fee simple, followed by a round of negotiations whereby some of the disputed property would be ceded to the other party. This elaborate ritual was destined, in a single move, to authenticate the absolute validity of the PRC claim to the territory in question, mollify the opponent through an act of formal transfer of a portion of the contested terrain to his name, and, ultima ratio, cast the Chinese in the enviable role of voluntary donors with the Soviets appearing throughout as mere recipients of unique Chinese generosity.

In subsequent reports, the PRC advocates began to pay greater attention to the job of spelling out the substance of their government's quarrel with the Soviets over the matter of the river islands in the context of the 1964 episode. Thus, on the occasion of the nationwide screening of the propaganda film, "The New Tsars' Anti-China Atrocities," the local mass media devoted considerable space to comment on a clip from the movie showing a "map handed to the Chinese side by the Soviet revisionists during the 1964 Sino-Soviet negotiations on the boundary question" as prima facie proof that the Soviets had "tampered with the boundary line as they pleased on this map and marked as their territory more than 600 of the over 700 islands on the Chinese side of the central lines of the channels of the Wusuli and Heilung Rivers."[11] Apart from illuminating the magnitude of the problem, the statement managed to convey the impression that the PRC authorities here endorsed once again the thalweg principle as the proper criterion for charting the boundary line between the two countries where it was pegged to a navigable river. To reinforce that contention, Peking afterwards declared that during the Sino-Soviet boundary negotiations in 1964, the Soviet representative, no less,

> also had to admit that the red line on the map attached to the "Sino-Russian Treaty of Peking" cannot show the precise alignment of the boundary line in the rivers, nor can it possibly determine the ownership of islands; he could not but agree that the central line of the main channel should be taken for determining the boundary line on the rivers and the ownership of islands.[12]

How correct this version of the proceedings is cannot be ascertained at this stage,[13] and only access to the minutes of the conference will provide the final answer. On balance, the claims made in the previously cited passages sound a trifle exaggerated, but not altogether unfounded.

THE 1964 AFFAIR: THE SOVIET SIDE

By contrast with the Chinese brief, which ranged far afield, the rival Soviet script in referring to the 1964 events has concentrated

THE 1964 CONFERENCE

exclusively on the theme of "minor border adjustments." This approach is quite understandable, since Moscow wanted to avoid at any cost getting entangled in endless polemics over the juridical respectability of the treaties that shaped the modern profile of the Sino-Soviet frontier and instead sought to narrow the meeting's agenda to an investigation of the prospects for implementing ad hoc "rectifications" of the existing boundary line in spots where technical modification in the previous modus operandi seemed advisable. But, where PRC sources paint a tableau of blind Soviet intransigence when asked to surrender a few random bits of "alien" soil, the Soviet official spokesmen's version of the story credits the Soviet Union with taking the initiative at the parley in submitting

> proposals whose adoption would have made it possible within the shortest period to carry out by mutual consent the specification of individual sectors of the Soviet-Chinese border line. The Soviet delegation was guided by the consideration that the successful completion of consultations would be an important contribution to maintaining friendly relations between our peoples and states.

The Chinese were therefore blamed for the breakdown of the 1964 negotiations and publicly attacked on the grounds that "the 1964 consultations showed that the Chinese side had no intention of reaching an agreement." Rather,

> the PRC delegation attempted to question the state border, which had been historically formed and confirmed by treaties. The Chinese side regarded the idea of the consultations as an opportunity of artificially creating "territorial problems" that would complicate relations between our peoples and countries for many years to come.[14]

THE 1964 CONFERENCE: FURTHER ANALYSIS

For all the impassioned oratory from both quarters, a careful reading of the record still leads one to believe that, in concrete terms, a very small distance separated the opponents and that, with a minimal effort, the remaining gap could easily have been bridged. Indeed, they themselves have acknowledged as much, since Peking as well as Moscow has often, as of late, openly said that it would "not have been difficult" to reach a settlement on that occasion, each, of course, interjecting that all that would have been necessary then to ensure the successful outcome of the talks was just the slightest display of inclination on the part of the other to behave sensibly and be willing to make no more than a token compromise. Or, as a recent Soviet communique summed it up:

> During the consultations in Peking in 1964 the Soviet side expressed its readiness to meet half way the wishes of the Chinese side, which were concerned with the interests of the Chinese population along the banks of the river, and to reach agreement on the demarcation of the frontier line between the Soviet Union and the People's Republic of China along the Rivers Amur and Ussuri on the basis of mutual concessions, on condition that the Chinese side, in its turn, showed a readiness to recognize correspondingly the interests of the Soviet population along particular sections of the frontier. This could have been a reasonable agreement based on a desire on the part of both sides to do away with tension and to maintain tranquility on the frontier.[15]

Thus, one has to discount as examples of post facto "poetic" license subsequent attributions of various extremist attitudes in conjunction with the history of the 1964 conference. For instance, Soviet authors have lately asserted that "the Chinese delegation made territorial claims against the Soviet Union declaring that tsarist Russia had allegedly seized over 1,540,000 square kilometers of Chinese land." The equation makes sense only if the Chinese references to the "unequal" character of the treaties which gave rise to the present configuration of the USSR-PRC frontier are gratuitously translated into an outright demand by the Chinese that the territory transferred by these agreements forthwith be restored to them. Available empirical evidence will not sustain the charge. Or, the Soviets have since read a sinister intent into the report that "the head of the Chinese delegation even pointed out that if the Soviet Union did not make concessions at the talks, the Chinese side 'may consider other ways of settling the question'."[16] Again, the Chinese may not have been making an overt threat at all, but serving notice that they were contemplating some more innocuous alternative, such as a unilateral declaration to the effect that the old frontier treaties were not just "unequal" but, hence, also null and void, or withdrawal of their previous offer to abide in practice by the current alignment of the frontier notwithstanding the invalidity of the underlying accords.

In a nutshell, what apparently torpedoed the 1964 session was not the issue of "territorial accommodations" per se, for both capitals profess, at least in retrospect, to have been prepared at the time to make the requisite sacrifices in order to forge a stable peace on their common frontier, nor is there any solid evidence to indicate that they did not mean what they assert. The mosaic, though fragmentary, thus suggests that the real stumbling block lay in the procedural instead of the substantive sphere and that the contestants might have arrived at a working consensus on the merits of the case without undue trouble had ideological factors not intruded into the conversations and doomed them to failure, namely: Peking's insistence on applying the ex cathedra formula by which all the old treaties relating to the Sino-Russian border first had to be pronounced "unequal," and next the PRC's title to the land "beyond the line established by these conventions" which allegedly had been subjected to Soviet occupation had to be redeemed; only then could businesslike discussions take place, a scenario to which the Soviets objected as a matter of sheer principle, more out of doctrinal than pragmatic motives. Hence, in the final analysis, the inability to reconcile the competing viewpoints on the question of diplomatic etiquette over the correct manner and suitable style of resolving the problem, rather than organic divergences of opinion with respect to the express terms of the settlement proper must be seen as the foremost cause of the political impasse which persists to this day.

The Norms of International Law

A significant aspect of this whole affair—which, in fact, fits nicely the thesis developed above—was the ethereal quality of the role played by the norms of international law on this occasion. In effect, the references to concrete "territorial encroachments" and the <u>thalweg</u> rule both raised issues that, in ordinary circumstances, are primarily governed by the standards of international law and, to that extent, injected a new legal theme into the Sino-Soviet dialogue concerning the frontier compared to the tenor of past exchanges and, furthermore, did so in quite explicit fashion, whereas heretofore the two parties seemed intent on avoiding such "specificity" on this touchy item. One might thus expect that since "juridical" topics had been broached, the tone of the discussions would reflect that move and switch to a more legalistic note. Yet, judging by the available evidence, this apparently did not occur, and the possible reasons for this singular phenomenon call for a closer look.

Consider first the problem of the territories which the Chinese then accused the Soviets of having usurped in disregard even of the dividing line fixed by the original treaties. This is the kind of charge which, if seriously meant, needs to be spelled out in careful detail in order to allow an intelligent appraisal on the merits and an appropriate solution, and that quintessential element is just what is conspicuously lacking in this case. At no point, to the best of our knowledge, have the Chinese submitted an authoritative listing of the extra pieces of real estate they claim to have been deprived of in violation of the provisions of the applicable agreements. The magnitude of the stake itself remains uncertain and a wide range of figures has been cited in this connection: 38,000 square kilometers; or 33,000 square kilometers (between 12,000 and 13,000 square miles in the Pamirs and islands in the Amur and Ussuri Rivers; or 21,000 square kilometers (20,000 in the Pamirs and 1,000 in border rivers).[17] Presumably, the Chinese do want some territorial adjustment in the existing profile of the Sino-Soviet frontier in their favor. However, as long as they fail to say exactly what they have in mind here and go on record with a bill of particularized demands, the impression will persist that the world is witnessing an academic debate in which the territorial theme serves extraneous ends and not a genuine dispute over ownership of designated acreage stricto sensu.

From what little we can tell, the 1964 meeting broke no new ground in that respect. A secondary (pro-Soviet) source has recently disclosed that when on that occasion the two sides exchanged maps

> examination of the Chinese maps revealed that they showed many sections of Soviet territory as belonging to China, while the frontier line over a considerable length was marked as passing inside Soviet territory beyond the line defined by the Russian-Chinese treaty documents and which has been guarded by Soviet frontier guards since the establishment of the Soviet state.
>
> Peking began pressing hard for the Soviet side to recognize the unilaterally compiled Chinese maps as legally valid before any examination of argument and counter-argument or of the Russian-Chinese treaty documents, in other words, to accept, a priori, the frontier line arbitrarily drawn on the Chinese maps.
>
> On the Chinese maps, parts of the Soviet territory between the existing frontier line and the line arbitrarily drawn by the Chinese side are presented as "areas in dispute"; at the same time Peking says that this term is a "concession" to the Soviet Union, intended to "ease" the Soviet Union's position and that, in fact, the "areas in dispute" are unquestionably Chinese territory.[18]

The account shed no light on how detailed these maps were and how much "Soviet" territory was reduced to the rank of "areas in dispute." Most important, even this partisan version managed to suggest that when the Chinese identified certain areas as "disputed," they did not take this to mean that all of that territory automatically had to be restored to PRC control, but sounded as though they were prepared to endorse some sort of modus vivendi which would parcel out these various lots. Again, this kind of ad hoc arrangement is a far cry from normal procedure under the circumstances and did nothing to dispel the doubts expressed earlier about the true motives behind the PRC bid in filing this claim.

Current Status of Contested Areas

Equally interesting was the stark neglect by either government to invoke the current status of the contested areas, although it is customary in a situation of this sort to rely on evidence of practical control to fortify one's legal position. Omission to take such a rudimentary precaution adds strength to the notion that both regimes still wished at this stage to steer clear of a direct legal confrontation. The result of this unusual reticence, though, is that the question of who actually had physical possession of the lands over which the PRC and the Soviet Union were now feuding or various chunks thereof was left officially unclarified. The general tendency was to assume that the Soviets occupied the areas to which the Chinese also claimed title and that the Chinese were trying to get them to vacate the inroads they had allegedly made by trespassing on soil which the old treaties had assigned to China.

Notwithstanding its earlier silence on that score, the Kremlin has certainly worked hard in recent years to correct the initial oversight and make use of every opportunity to publicize the idea that all of this ground has always been under the effective jurisdiction of the Soviet state, with special emphasis on conditions along the fluvial stretches of the border. Soviet sources dip into history, for example, to make the point that, after overrunning Manchuria, the Japanese attempted "to capture islands on the Amur and the Ussuri belonging to the Soviet Union. . .which became at times the scene of serious armed encounters where the Japanese aggressors were given a crushing rebuff."[19] Another common pitch is that

> the Chinese authorities showed interest in using several Soviet islands on the Ussuri and Amur rivers for economic and production purposes (the procuring of hay, wood, and so on), in providing Chinese fishermen with the opportunity of fishing in the Soviet part of the rivers. For this they addressed competent Soviet authorities for permission. Their requests were favorably considered and satisfied by the Soviet side. The procedure of asking for

the use of Soviet islands and the Soviet part of the rivers which was observed by the Chinese authorities for many years is one of the proofs that the Chinese side never questioned the fact that the above islands, Damansky Island included, belonged to the Soviet Union.[20]

By contrast, the PRC's attitude has been less consistent. As previously mentioned, at first Peking's policy seemed to be aimed at rolling the Soviets back from their advanced position. To the extent, for instance, that the Chinese were then advocating a return to the thalweg (for example, in their note of August 23, 1963), the obvious conclusion was that they alone had something to gain from that formula which, in turn, meant that the Soviets had gone beyond that line and were holding the ground lying in the strip between the middle of the main channel and the outer reaches of the control perimeter manned by Soviet local authorities nearer to the PRC's bank. Much later, the Chinese too woke up to the significant advantages accruing from the ability to argue adverse possession and they have since made a concerted, if belated, effort to erase the earlier image and persuade all and sundry that already "after the conclusion of the 'Sino-Russian Treaty of Peking,' the two sides always took the central line of the main channel for determining the ownership of the islands and exercised jurisdiction accordingly."[21]

At any rate, the important thing to note here is that the kind of claim both countries are not at all averse to airing in this connection at present, neither of them was apparently prepared to press back in 1964, notwithstanding the strict privacy of the conference room. Was it because the fate of these fragments of land was incidental to the main thrust of the debates and so did not warrant sufficient attention to call for a thorough exploration of these issues? Or was it because resorting to the technicalities of the law in this situation was not yet considered proper in light of the prescribed code of behavior between socialist nations, even when discussing the matter in camera? On each count, the answer may well be affirmative.

The Thalweg

With the business of the thalweg, the picture is rather more complicated. To begin with, there are indications that the problem, looked at in retrospect, has a longer history than one initially had reason to suspect. The observation stems from the recent controversy around the passage in Article 1 of the Sino-Soviet agreement on the regime of navigation on border waterways of 1951 to the effect that navigation by ships of either country on border waterways follows the main navigable channel "regardless of where the line of the state frontier runs."[22] The Soviet side has claimed that the statement constituted a formal recognition of the concept that the boundary line need not coincide with the thalweg and that, indeed, in this case it did not.[23] The Chinese bluntly retort that this accord is "in no sense a treaty or agreement for the settlement of the boundary question."[24] Both parties have a valid point. The Chinese are quite right in asserting that the 1951 convention did not fix the location of the boundary line between the Soviet Union and the PRC on the Amur, Ussuri, Argun, and Sungacha Rivers and on Lake Khanka. By the same token, the Soviets are correct in emphasizing that the document in question drew a difference between the two phenomena. Thus, while the text of the agreement did not flatly say that the boundary line did not in fact retrace the thalweg or confirm expressis verbis that the boundary line was situated elsewhere than along the thalweg, nevertheless it also plainly acknowledged the possibility that the two might diverge.

On balance, then, the wording of the clause can only be described as ambiguous, as though Moscow and Peking were eager to settle the practical topic of the navigation routes without getting bogged down in the difficult subject of the position of the corresponding stretch of their shared frontier. The implication is that the formula they chose to use on this occasion represented a deliberate compromise designed to paper over a lack of consensus on or perhaps mere uncertainty as to where the local boundary line lay or ought to lie. Absent an agreement on that score, the Soviets and the Chinese apparently decided to skip the matter altogether and proceed instead to take care of the immediate task of defining the mechanics of joint utilization of the border streams. The ambivalent way in which the affair was handled, however, does strongly suggest that even at that early date the location of the fluvial sector of the frontier had proved a sticky wicket for the socialist duo to negotiate, despite their constant and vocal professions meanwhile of mutual friendship and fraternal affinity.

The record of how the thalweg question fared at the 1964 conference fuels further speculation. As previously mentioned, the Chinese later declared that the Soviet spokesmen at the meeting openly conceded that the boundary line in the border rivers had to follow the middle of the main navigable channel. Official Soviet media subsequently indicated that on that occasion the competent Soviet representatives had expressed a willingness to compromise on the issue and make whatever adjustments might prove mutually satisfactory, but have never explicitly either admitted or denied the gist of the PRC's version. However, secondary (Soviet and pro-Soviet) sources have done so. One Soviet author has let it be known that during these negotiations the "Soviet side showed readiness to meet the wishes of the Chinese side and reach agreement on tracing the boundary line between the Soviet Union and the PRC in the border sections of the Amur and Ussuri rivers along the main navigable channel."[25] Meanwhile, a Polish scribe, obviously fronting for the Soviets, has leaked a rather more elaborate story. According to him:

> A curious fact is that the Chinese invariably complain that the Chinese-Soviet border on the rivers does not run along the channel. But the truth is that the eastern river border, in particular along the Amur and Ussuri, goes where it was fixed by the Russian-Chinese treaty documents of 1858-60. Yet when the Soviet Union proposes that the frontier line on the border parts of the rivers should be drawn along the channel, the Chinese reject these proposals or bring them to nothing by their actions.
>
> During the Soviet-Chinese consultations on border issues in 1964, preliminary agreement was reached at working group level on almost the entire eastern part of the border. The sides agreed to fix the border on the navigable rivers along the fairway, and on the non-navigable along the middle of the rivers.[26]

Without buying either the Soviet or the PRC's account of who actually said and did what at the 1964 conference, one can nevertheless safely conclude that at some point then the Soviets had for practical purposes endorsed the thalweg principle as suitable grounds on which to resolve Sino-Soviet differences over the geographical location of the frontier at the extreme end of their common perimeter. Technical questions aside, the bare fact that Khrushchev was now prepared to make that compromise when only the preceding summer he had flatly rejected a PRC suggestion to adopt the thalweg rule attested to the current sense of desperation in the Kremlin councils finally to bury this unfortunate business with a minimum of delay, provided the price was acceptable. The projected arrangement fit that requirement and apparently at this juncture that was enough for the present leadership to acquiesce in the proposed scheme.

An interesting aspect of the affair, once again, was the absence of any sign that attempts were made to resort to the instrumentalities of international law in a situation that prima facie qualified for precisely that brand of analysis. A possible explanation is that the Soviets, having decided to make the "sacrifice," simply did not want to cause fresh complications by starting a legal debate. Yet, they could still have mounted a legal defense of the status quo, without fear of unduly jeopardizing the prospects of the kind of settlement they already had in mind, and, having made their point, then could have graciously gone on to embrace the new modus vivendi. Certainly, in the ordinary course of events, such a procedure has much to recommend it and so a brief pause to examine why the usual routine was not followed in this instance may be justified.

For, it must be remembered that a meaningful appeal to the canon of international law was quite warranted by the data in the case and that, indeed, the artifacts of international law have since been pressed into service for that purpose. Thus, the Soviet government's statement of June 13, 1969, sought to refer to the record of international legal practice in support of its contention that states had at various times placed the boundary line in navigable border waterways elsewhere than in the middle of the <u>thalweg</u>, which, Moscow claimed, is the formula which was also applied in 1861 to some stretches of the Ussuri River. To quote the relevant passage:

> It is generally known that in international law there does not exist a standard automatically establishing the frontier on border rivers as passing along the middle of the river's main stream. When concluding appropriate treaties the states delineate the border as appears to them most suitable in accordance with circumstances. There are examples in interstate relations in which the border has been established along the bank of a river, and not in midstream.
>
> The 1858 treaty between Costa Rica and Nicaragua provides that the frontier line passes along the right bank of the River San Juan and "the Republic of Nicaragua has the exclusive right of possession and sovereign jurisdiction over the waters of that river." A similar delimitation of frontiers along rivers is found in agreements between other countries.
>
> The 1860 Russo-Chinese Treaty of Peking is another such example. An admission of the fact that the frontier line does not necessarily coincide with the mainstream was reflected in the Soviet-Chinese agreement regulating navigation on frontier rivers which was concluded in 1951. Article 1 of the agreement says that the navigation of vessels of both sides on frontier rivers is effected along the mainstream, "irrespective of where the line of the state frontier passes."[27]

The Soviet bid elicited the following Chinese reply:

> In order to deny the principle of international law that the central line of the main channel shall form the boundary line in the case of navigable boundary rivers, the Soviet Government cited as an example the treaty concluded between Costa Rica and Nicaragua in 1858, saying

that this treaty stipulates that "the boundary line" between Costa Rica and Nicaragua "runs along the right bank of the San Juan River" and that "the Republic of Nicaragua enjoys exclusive right of possession and sovereign jurisdiction over the waters of this river"; moreover, it impudently alleged that the "Sino-Russian Treaty of Peking" was likewise a case in point. Of course, there are exceptions to any established principle of international law, and the same is true of the principle that the central line of the main channel shall form the boundary in the case of navigable boundary rivers. But explicit stipulations must be made in treaties for any exceptional case. Articles II and VI of the 1858 boundary treaty between Costa Rica and Nicaragua do contain such stipulations. Now we want to ask the Soviet Government: Where is it stipulated in the "Sino-Russian Treaty of Peking" that the boundary line between China and Russia runs along the Chinese bank of the Heilung and Wusuli Rivers? And where is it stipulated that tsarist Russia "enjoys exclusive right of possession and sovereign jurisdiction over the Heilung and Wusuli Rivers?"[28]

The technical merits of the respective positions are not the key problem here, except perhaps to note that neither party succeeded in the course of this exchange to set forth an unassailable claim. Rather, to emphasize an earlier observation, the importance of these two excerpts resides in the fact that they illustrate that respectable arguments drawn from the repertory of international law were readily available to both contestants and yet neither of them chose to use that weapon in 1964. Apart from the motivation mentioned before that the Soviets might have preferred not to drag the matter out by further discussions now that they had reconciled themselves to the idea of having to recognize the thalweg principle, another reason could well be that at this stage of the game both Moscow and Peking still hesitated to inject the process of international law into an intramural dialogue. What maybe was permissible after the incidence of bloodshed in 1969 and at a time when relations between the Soviet Union and the PRC were no longer defined by the terms of socialist internationalism apparently was not felt to be appropriate in 1964 when, at least formally, the old rules continued to operate. To be sure, the thalweg phenomenon itself is a legal concept, but it entered the picture in an almost perfunctory way and seemingly without benefit of legal elaboration. Judging by available information, the Chinese acted as though the validity and relevance of the thalweg rule were unimpeachable and made no special effort to justify that proposition, thus keeping the legal presence to an absolute minimum.

THE 1964 CONFERENCE

In addition, one should consider the possibility that at this juncture the Soviets might have had grave doubts about the wisdom of openly opposing the _thalweg_ principle in favor of a practice whose antecedents were doctrinally impure and which even they had had occasion to drop from their diplomatic portfolio. For example, on June 13, 1946, the Soviet Union and Afghanistan signed an agreement on border questions which, inter alia, established that the line of the state frontier between them on the Amu-Darya River and the navigable portion of the Pyandzh River would follow the _thalweg_; where the location of the _thalweg_ could not be determined, the line of the frontier would follow the middle of the main navigable channel of each waterway and, in the non-navigable section of the Pyandzh, it would pass in the middle of the stream.[29] These arrangements superseded a deal worked out between tsarist Russia and England back in the nineteenth century which had given the former title and control over these border streams right up to the opposite, that is, Afghan, bank and had excluded Afghanistan from access to their waters.[30] Presumably, these vestiges of an imperialist past now caused some embarrassment and a more equitable solution was devised which conformed to general precedent whereby the Soviet Union "voluntarily and gratis" restored to Afghanistan rights of which it had been "unfairly" deprived. Indeed, an accompanying telegram from the prime minister of Afghanistan to Stalin in connection with the conclusion of the agreement took particular note of this gesture of friendship and justice on the part of the Soviet Union, as though to underscore that this enlightened act served to redress an ancient wrong and represented a triumph for legitimacy.[31]

Under the circumstances, the task of figuring out alibis for behaving differently—and less generously—toward "socialist" China probably radiated little attraction and this feature, too, could help explain why the Soviet leaders sounded so amenable to accepting the _thalweg_ principle in 1964 without raising any fuss over the issue.[32]

The Soviet Impetus

In the context of what we know of the 1964 experiment, one further conclusion recommends itself: the practical impetus for summoning the colloquy stemmed from the Kremlin. The Soviets traveled to Peking for that purpose. They subsequently showed interest in keeping the border commission alive, while the Chinese apparently could not have cared whether that body functioned or not. Given the past history of the dispute, the switch in the Soviet attitude can be described only as dramatic. Neither party has ever supplied a formal explanation of these events, but a few conjectures may be ventured that might account for the startling reversal of roles in the marathon diplomatic tournament foreshadowed by this episode.

Looking back, it would seem that Khrushchev had here miscalculated rather badly from the very outset. The decision to inject the territorial theme into the Sino-Soviet dialogue had, on balance, quite obviously boomeranged. True, Peking's reflex to Khrushchev's jibe on its failure to "liberate" Hong Kong and Macao had furnished Moscow with the opportunity to denounce the Chinese as "territorial revisionists" for their pejorative references to the legal status of the Sino-Soviet border, and the fortuitous Himalayan affair added fuel to the flames. In the long haul, however, the results of the foray had proved disappointing. The Chinese had refused to be stampeded into any rash pronouncements or actions that would lend sustenance to the charge that the PRC regime was bent on physical expansion across its northern perimeter. The dust soon settled on the frontier with India as well, with the Chinese again betraying no desire to annex Indian soil beyond the contested zone, even after its occupation by the People's Liberation Army (PLA).

On the other hand, now that the Soviet leadership had publicly broached the subject (either of its own volition or in a fit of temper following persistent, though insidious, goading by the Chinese at the diplomatic level and petty agitation on the frontier itself), the PRC hierarchy could and did use that lever to exert enough pressure on its ally to annoy and disturb Soviet official circles: symbolic provocations and demonstrative probes at the border irritated the Soviets, and yet no matter how hard Moscow broadcasted these incidents, they sounded too puny in scope and significance to really hurt the PRC's image abroad. Plus, the Kremlin never managed to adduce any concrete evidence that the PRC's behavior in the Siberian and Central Asian border regions was indeed intended to alter by force the configuration of the existing frontier. The desolate river islands might constitute an exception in this respect, but the title to them was sufficiently beclouded for the Soviet charge of PRC aggressiveness in their sporadic endeavors to exercise rights of possession on these scattered shreds of land to stick. By then, inveighing against the Chinese for having let the Sino-Indian border quarrel degenerate into a shooting war also was like flogging a dead horse: that unpleasantness had blown over, the neighboring countries wanted to forget the upheaval, and the Indians themselves probably preferred not to be reminded that their impotency alone prevented them from recouping their fortunes.

Khrushchev had thus unloosed a Frankenstein and reaped no tangible reward for his efforts; rather, he was currently paying a political price out of all proportion to the visible gains. Introducing the territorial issue had undoubtedly aggravated the controversy with the PRC and had come dangerously close to transforming a doctrinal

THE 1964 CONFERENCE

duel into a state confrontation. The ideological conflict between the two capitals had noticeably worsened as of late, and unhappiness with Khrushchev's handling of this situation, among the rest, was beginning to mount at home.

In the light of the above, the pilgrimage to Peking was undertaken, at a guess, in pursuit of one of twin objectives. The primary goal was to put the monster Khrushchev had fathered safely back under wraps with a minimum of advertisement and without undue "loss of face." The trip itself amounted to a placatory gesture; having failed to get the Chinese to cooperate in issuing a joint press announcement of the impending conference, the Soviets perhaps planned not to air the matter in advance altogether, and the Chinese proceeded to mention it first. If a satisfactory deal were sealed, Khrushchev would have presumably faced the domestic opposition with a fait accompli, taken personal credit for disposing of a difficult problem, and hoped to emerge the victor in the looming intramural struggle for power. If the attempt missed, Khrushchev could still have tried to salvage his career by launching a full-scale attack on the Communist Chinese for their intransigence and, by identifying his rivals in the Politburo with the Peking faction, sought to portray them as enemies of Soviet national interests and so blocked their bid for control. In either case, the game had to be played with consummate finesse. A positive solution would have to be achieved on terms that could be presented to his disgruntled associates as a vindication of his prior policy line vis-a-vis Peking, and the Chinese would be sure to checkmate any move designed to redeem Khrushchev's prestige at their expense. In the event of a negative outcome, the blame would somehow have to be placed on the shoulders of the mainland regime, and that would not be easy either, considering that the PRC's contribution to the flow of oratory on the Sino-Soviet frontier question had struck throughout a note of remarkable moderation and restraint.

The PRC's Response

In the end, of course, the gambit failed. One suspects that the Chinese knew of Khrushchev's troubles, for barely had the Soviet and PRC spokesmen sat down to business than the Central Committee of the Chinese Communist Party saw fit to dispatch a public letter to its Soviet alter ego which spelled out afresh the PRC's views on various aspects of their simmering border feud. The message purveyed a masterly blend of tactfulness-cum-intractability. With an eye to the round of frontier talks that had just opened, the communication began by recalling that

> the Government of the People's Republic of China has
> consistently held that the question of the boundary between
> China and the Soviet Union, which is a legacy from the past,
> can be settled through negotiation between the two Govern-
> ments. It has also held that, pending such a settlement, the
> status quo on the border should be maintained.[33]

On the one hand, the statement was a perfectly accurate description of the official PRC position on this particular subject up till then, with which nobody could cavil in good faith. On the other, the words plainly implied, as they must have been meant to, that the current discussions fully validated Peking's thesis on this issue.

Not content with this bit of self-congratulation though, the Communist Chinese next tried to pin on the Soviet comrades the responsibility for the present crisis in their frontier relations. Insisting that "this is what we have done over the past ten years or more [that is, maintained the status quo on the border]" and that "had the Soviet Government taken the same attitude, both sides could have lived in amity along the border and preserved tranquility there," Peking charged that

> with the stepping up of anit-Chinese activities by the
> leaders of the CPSU in recent years, the Soviet side has
> made frequent breaches of the status quo on the border,
> occupied Chinese territory, and provoked border incidents.
> Still more serious, the Soviet side has flagrantly carried
> out large-scale subversive activities in Chinese frontier
> areas, trying to sow discord among China's nationalities
> by means of the press and wireless, inciting China's minor-
> ity nationalities to break away from their motherland,
> and inveigling and coercing tens of thousands of Chinese
> citizens into going to the Soviet Union. Not only do all
> these acts violate the principles guiding relations between
> socialist countries, they are absolutely impermissible even
> in the relations between countries in general.[34]

The bulk of the PRC's allegations of Soviet meddling in Sinkiang and elsewhere rang true. The rest of the accusations, however, lacked credibility. This applies especially to the assertion that the Soviets "made frequent breaches of the status quo on the border, occupied Chinese territory, and provoked border incidents." Not only is there no documented evidence to support this indictment (save perhaps in connection with the midstream islands), but the claim looked suspiciously like a clumsy attempt to tar the Soviets with their own brush.

The proposition that the Soviets encouraged the PRC's ethnic minorities to secede from the PRC seems equally far-fetched. More to the point is the fact that the Chinese chose to bring up the topic at this late date and, according to press accounts, the PRC and Soviet delegates assembled in Peking were expected to deal with it too, for the Soviets meanwhile were striving to sound as conciliatory as possible on that score. Typical of the new attitude were the contemporary remarks attributed to the Chairman of the Council of Ministers of the Kirghiz Soviet Socialist Republic who, confirming that many people had entered Kirghizia and Kazakhstan from Sinkiang in the preceding months, amplified on the comment by explaining that "several requests were made to the Chinese to prevent this 'mass flow' of people," that those who had migrated into Soviet territory were assigned proper jobs and "economically placed exactly" as Soviet citizens, and that the exodus had since stopped.[35]

The net impression is that the Soviets were trying to wiggle off the hook, as gracefully as circumstances would allow, and the Chinese would have none of it. In similar vein, seeing that Moscow had more than once sought to buttress its case against Peking by invoking the universal norms of international behavior, the latter seized the occasion to reciprocate by promptly adjudging the Kremlin's conduct in this domain to have fallen short of the standards regulating the mode of transaction not merely between "fraternal nations" but between any random pair of countries on earth, whatever their political complexion.

The pattern persisted. The Chinese again borrowed a page from Khrushchev's script. The Soviets had freely used the Indian affair to castigate the Chinese and so the Chinese forthwith proceeded to repay them in kind with the cogent observation that

> among all our neighbors it is only the leaders of the CPSU and the reactionary nationalists of India who have deliberately created border disputes with China. The Chinese Government has satisfactorily settled complicated boundary questions, which were legacies from the past, both with all its fraternal socialist neighbors except the Soviet Union, and with its nationalist neighbors such as Burma, Nepal, Pakistan and Afghanistan, with the exception of India.[36]

These were telling blows and, in the opinion of many, Peking may well have had the best of the argument. Khrushchev had diligently paraded the example of India in an effort to tarnish the PRC's reputation on the world scene and the Chinese in this instance neatly demonstrated how the Soviets could be hoisted with their own petard. Having publicly associated themselves with the Indians in their grievances against the Chinese, the Soviets were also forced to share with them the dubious distinction of standing virtually alone in bearing that burden when every other state around the PRC's continental rim had already managed to strike a profitable territorial bargain with it. Invidious comparisons can cut both ways. They did here, at any rate, and not to Moscow's great advantage either.

Then came the clincher. After corroborating reports that "the delegations of our two Governments started boundary negotiations in Peking on February 25, 1964," the Communist Chinese let all and sundry know, as they had just finished informing the Soviets in camera, that

> although the old treaties relating to the Sino-Russian boundary are unequal treaties, the Chinese Government is nevertheless willing to respect them and take them as the basis for a reasonable settlement of the Sino-Soviet boundary question. Guided by proletarian internationalism and the principles governing relations between socialist countries, the Chinese Government will conduct friendly negotiations with the Soviet Government in the spirit of consultation on an equal footing and mutual understanding and mutual accommodation. If the Soviet side takes the same attitude as the Chinese Government, the settlement of the Sino-Soviet boundary question, we believe, ought not to be difficult, and the Sino-Soviet boundary will truly become one of lasting friendship.[37]

In short, the Chinese spoke softly, yet on the essentials they refused to yield an inch. As hitherto, what they wanted was a formal clarification of the location of the entire Sino-Soviet boundary line. The Soviets either had to accept that cardinal premise or look forward to returning to Moscow empty-handed. Granted, even after the original compromise, they could end up manning a frontier with the PRC more or less identical with the existing one, but for that they would thenceforth be indebted to Peking's magnanimity. An analogous border trace would be the product of special dispensation on the part of the Chinese Communists and not a recognition of the local title purportedly acquired by the Russians by dint of the ancient treaties imposed on China by the tsarist empire. Moreover, once that Pandora's box was unlocked, who could guarantee the Kremlin that Peking would still not advance further conditions, when the lid could not be snapped shut and after the status quo had been hopelessly jeopardized?

Such an abject psychological surrender and the corporeal risks involved were too much for the Soviets to swallow, no matter how badly they might have wished to put an end to the border "vendetta."

THE 1964 CONFERENCE

For Khrushchev personally, the worst aspect of the whole affair was that the Chinese had decisively outmaneuvered him. He had not been able to budge them and, at the same time, their response had been articulated in language so constructive and sensible as to deprive him of an opportunity to cast them persuasively in the role of villains. Furthermore, the Soviets had been closemouthed about the conference, and the Chinese had stolen a march on them by releasing their version of the story first, complete with optimistic predictions and a happy solution. Propaganda-wise, Khrushchev had suffered a serious defeat. Lastly, the very sins imputed to him were those he had previously laid at Peking's doorstep, nor could he counter that the Chinese were thus escalating the dispute or spreading lies since earlier he had accused them of the same crimes and had set a precedent by not bothering to furnish evidence to substantiate the charges. Often nothing hurts more than, or is so hard to handle as, a canard coming home to roost. Khrushchev must have found the experience singularly unpalatable.

The Chinese Take the Initiative

At this point, the initiative here passed to the Communist Chinese. Mutual recriminations in this area, momentarily interrupted, revived, but the zest was gone. Stock denunciations were traded listlessly, the chorus lapsed into a tired refrain. The Soviet Consul General in Calcutta criticized the PRC hierarchy for "indulging in adventurism and provoking border incidents with neighboring countries" and recited the staple formula that "the violations of the Soviet border by the Chinese in 1962 and 1963 were a constant occurrence" and that "sometimes this took the form of flagrant provocations."[38] An eminent Soviet international jurist is quoted as having declared that

> no territorial questions exist between the Soviet Union and the PRC and that the Soviet-Chinese frontier had taken shape historically. The only question can be one of separate clarifications of the frontier, which are necessary. But the Chinese side has for some time been continually and systematically violating the Soviet-Chinese frontier and, furthermore, frequently in a crude and provocative manner.

The legal expert's conclusion was that this "is in flagrant contradiction of the generally accepted standards of law."[39] The Chinese flailed away at recent Soviet tactics in Sinkiang, and the Soviets scored the Chinese for conspiring to exploit the proletariat of Hong Kong and of betraying the goals of revolution by bolstering the colony's capitalist economy.[40]

Even border incidents recurred while the conference was officially in session. Thus, on May 3, 1964, forty Chinese with two tractors reportedly violated the USSR state frontier near the settlement of Bakhty (on the Kazakh Soviet Socialist Republic-Sinkiang border) and started plowing a section of Soviet terrain. The demand of the Soviet frontier guards that they quit Soviet soil was met by an outburst of hooliganism: the trespassers shoved the guards, drove the tractors at them, and so on. Then, on June 13, a group of 60 Chinese citizens in 26 boats and launches entered Soviet waters in the Amur River. When approached by a Soviet patrol boat, the intruders began waving sticks and oars, threatening the crew of the patrol boat and the members of the frontier guard unit, trying to push the guards into the water.[41] This sense of déjà vu also extended to the plane of high diplomacy: on June 30, 1964, in Ulan-Bator, at the third session of the Sino-Mongolian joint commission for the demarcation of the frontier, a final protocol was signed. According to a current Soviet interpretation, "this step of the Chinese leadership was connected less with its aims with respect to the MPR than with the question of its large territorial claims toward the Soviet Union" which, the Soviets point out, were voiced soon after. Presumably, the Chinese had acted in anticipation of their next move, calculating that "the treaty consolidation of the frontier with the MPR would serve to confirm that, as a champion of justice, Peking could not come out with groundless territorial demands" vis-a-vis, say, the Soviet Union.[42]

Both dialogue and practice led nowhere—a plateau had been reached. This state of suspended animation could, conceivably, have lingered on. Khrushchev had shot his bolt. Having in effect won the match, the Chinese could at this juncture let the subject drop or move to administer the coup de grâce. Mao chose the latter path, and in July 1964, in the course of an interview with a Japanese socialist delegation visiting Peking, the deed was done.[43]

PRC CLAIMS ARE RAISED AT AN OFFICIAL PUBLIC LEVEL

The choice of terminal points for the periodization of the history of Sino-Soviet polemics on the territorial theme poses some difficulties. The 1969 clashes on the Amur and Ussuri Rivers present one possibility in that resort to force automatically stamps the incident as a dramatic departure from the preceding pattern of activity in this sphere. Yet, on closer examination, it turns out that in strictly diplomatic terms, that is, disregarding the egregious element of violence, the interview granted by Mao to a group of Japanese socialists on July 10, 1964, marks a crucial watershed in the thrust and tenor of the bilateral exchanges on the border topic and thus constitutes a better signpost for purposes of temporal demarcation than the 1969 events.

In effect, going by Mao's reported remarks, the question of territorial claims against the Soviet Union was for the first time explicitly raised in public at an official level. In all previous cases where the subject had been touched upon, the situation either involved concrete statements concerning territorial adjustments which were kept private and only leaked out many years later or open, but indeterminate, references to discrepancies in the current configuration of the Sino-Soviet frontier that should be attended to in due course. Mao's readiness now to charge the Soviets with specific misdeeds in the manner of acquisition of various portions of their territorial domain and his willingness to voice these accusations in a context where their world-wide dissemination was guaranteed stands in stark contrast with past practice here and set the tone for subsequent debates over this issue.

However, care was still taken to preserve formal appearances. For instance, the contents of Mao's talk with the visiting Japanese delegation were never featured in any mainland source. Presumably, the item was too touchy for such a direct approach and having the story emanate from a third party maintained the air of aloofness from crass property squabbles which socialist nations have sought to cultivate. In addition, the technique had some tangible advantages. To the extent that the account originated abroad, its accuracy could be impugned at some future date, if need be. Failure to publicize Mao's comments at home also meant that they were not elevated to the status of a firm policy commitment and saved the PRC leadership the trouble of then having to institute suitable action to vindicate the views expressed on that occasion. To repudiate the Chairman's words by a passive attitude on the territorial affair or to run the high risk of provoking a clash with the Soviets by following his dicta did not look especially attractive, and this roundabout way of making one's pitch while avoiding the worst of the potentially unpleasant consequences offered a fine alternative.

Nevertheless, the Soviets in their response brushed the pretense aside. Their retort, in the form of a lengthy Pravda editorial, was aimed directly at the Chinese and proceeded on the assumption that the statements attributed to Mao in the Japanese press correctly reproduced what he had said in conversation with his Japanese guests.[44] Whether the Chinese were being subtle or careful in preferring the circuitous route, the Soviets would have none of it and, at least in terms of selecting the channels of communication, treated the matter as something they wished squarely to confront the Chinese with. By so doing, they rejected the tacit PRC invitation to let the whole business retain a private flavor and worsened the situation by putting the harsher PRC demands on record instead of allowing them the quasi-anonymity for which deliberate PRC discretion seemed to slate them, in which position their capacity to spark conflict would be drastically reduced. Moscow's decision to meet the issue head-on may be a reliable index to the intensity of its frustration in the face of the tactics used by the Chinese and the degree of its inability to get the Chinese to work on solving the routine aspects of the frontier question. A sense of quickening desperation may in fact have led Khrushchev to lash out publicly at what he perceived as the latest installment in the campaign of elusive harassment that the Chinese had successfully waged against him all these years through stealthy promotion of the theme of "territorial accommodation."

The second novel feature of these discussions lay in the conscious PRC effort to instigate other states to press territorial claims against the Soviet Union, with mention, apart from Japan, of Rumania, East Germany, Poland, and Finland as countries that had unjustifiably lost territory to the Soviet Union at different times and ostensibly were entitled to seek the return of land which the Soviets had seized from them. The appeal to various neighbors of the Soviet Union to push for a favorable revision of their existing frontiers with the Soviet Union represented a critical shift in the style of conduct that the Chinese had hitherto pursued in this sector. Indeed, if any single element of Mao's performance in this instance was calculated to enrage the Soviets, the attempt to incite allies of the Soviet Union such as Rumania, East Germany, and Poland, and, even more, former enemies like Japan and Finland, to agitate for the recarving of large stretches of the Soviet Union's postwar boundaries to their own benefit would amply serve the purpose and the episode could then explain the strident tone and ad hominem character of the Kremlin's reaction.

What is more, according to the Soviets, the bid was prepared well in advance and does not amount to an isolated phenomenon that can be excused as a spontaneous afterthought or an ad hoc improvisation. Rather, they contend, systematic exploration of the terrain preceded the final move. To quote one version of the alleged behind-the-scenes maneuvers:

> During the Soviet-Chinese negotiations on cultural ties which took place in February, 1963, the Chinese side evinced heightened interest in certain Union and Autonomous republics of the Soviet Union—Moldavia, Latvia, Lithuania, Estonia, and Karelia.
> Two months prior to these negotiations (in December, 1962), acting on instructions from above, the secretary

of the Union of Chinese musicians, Li Yuan-tsin, on the
innocent pretext of "interest in music" tried to reach
agreement with Soviet cultural figures to obtain materials relating to "peoples part of whom live on the territory of the PRC and the other part live within the borders
of the USSR, in areas contiguous to Sinkiang," in whom
"the Chinese comrades were very interested."

The Chinese personnel who soon after arrived in the
Soviet Union pursuant to the plans of cultural cooperation
persistently sought to visit these regions of the Soviet
Union. Such interest was not accidental. Its true motives
became clear a little later from Mao Tse-tung's talks
with the Japanese socialists, which took place in August,
1964, in which Mao Tse-tung came out with an attempt
to manufacture so-called territorial questions between
socialist countries, to undermine the friendship and
cooperation of the peoples of socialist countries.

As far as the interest in "peoples part of whom live
on the territory of the PRC and the other part live within
the borders of the Soviet Union, in areas contiguous to
Sinkiang" is concerned, it found expression in the notorious territorial claims of the Mao Tse-tung group against
the Soviet Union.[45]

The Soviet interpretation of PRC intentions enjoyed some support
among informed foreign observers as well, especially as regards
sundry contemporary developments in relations between the Soviet
Union and Rumania, although opinions differed on the magnitude of
the PRC role in this affair, that is, whether Peking simply exploited
earlier tensions between Moscow and Bucharest over the status of
Bessarabia or helped fabricate the controversy. In the view of a
number of Western observers, the Rumanians deserved sole credit
for reviving the Bessarabian issue and, for example, one leading
expert on East European affairs surveying the local picture from the
vantage point of 1966 analyzed the situation without once referring to
the "Chinese connection." From his account:

Two years ago [i.e., in 1964] there were rumors that
Bucharest's leaders had secretly asked Moscow for return
of the territory taken in 1940. There have been signs
recently that the leaders of the Soviet Republic of Moldavia
have been alarmed at what they regard as the effort made
in Rumania to stir nationalist feelings among the roughly
two million Rumanians living in the Soviet area that was
formerly Bessarabia. Bucharest has gone to some trouble

to put on the historic record the fact that Karl Marx
thought the area in question properly belonged to Rumania,
not Russia.

The issue raised in all this goes much further than the
Rumanian claims. The broader question is the fate of all
the territorial gains the Soviet Union made first as the
fruit of Stalin's alliance with Hitler, and later as a victor
in World War II.

The same kind of case Rumania makes for getting back
Bessarabia and northern Bukovina could also be made by
Latvians, Estonians and Lithuanians to demand their independence and the undoing of their forced incorporation into
the Soviet Union. The Poles could call for the return of the
territory they lost in 1939 when Hitler and Stalin partitioned that oft-dismembered land. From Prague could
come a demand for return of the Carpatho-Ukraine. East
Germans could suggest Moscow give back the former
Königsberg area.[46]

By contrast, Japanese spokesmen have tended to portray the
PRC as a vital catalyst in stiffening the resolve of the Soviet Union's
East European allies, principally Rumania, to seek "territorial compensations" from their Soviet partner, as witness the following press
commentary:

In eastern Europe, moreover, it is reported from some
quarters that Rumania, which is beginning to follow an
"independent line," has asked the Soviet Union for reversion of the Bessarabian area. It is rumored that, if this
is true, the USSR may be in a tight spot, particularly
because similar problems exist with Poland and Czechoslovakia. The point to be noted particularly at this time is
that Chairman Mao reportedly revealed that Rumania has
resisted Moscow ever since the Chinese side fully explained
its stand to the Rumanian delegation, including Premier
Maurer, when it visited Peking to mediate the Sino-Soviet
conflict. It can be said that this statement virtually confirms the fact that Peking has openly aggravated the friction between the Soviet Union and Eastern Europe on the
territorial question.[47]

At any rate, Mao's pronouncements on this fateful occasion quite
obviously operated to inject a new dimension into the Sino-Soviet territorial debate that was destined to become a regular fixture of subsequent diplomatic exchanges between the two regimes pertaining to

THE 1964 CONFERENCE 123

the configuration of their shared national frontier. The Soviets promptly adopted the PRC's technique and have tried to repay the Chinese in their own coin by sicking some of the adjoining states on the PRC in connection with unsettled border disputes that cropped up in their relations with the PRC. Mongolia, as already indicated, has been a prime object of this tender "solicitude." Several incidents featuring Mongolia were noted earlier in charting the course of the Sino-Soviet polemics over the profile of their common boundary, but the Soviets have since gone back and combed their files for additional cases suggesting PRC hegemonial aspirations in their dealings with Mongolia in the recent past. As an example of what the process involves, the Soviets have attributed sinister motives to Peking's proposal in 1956 to extend material aid to Mongolia by supplying that country with "a large quantity of workers," a plan which reportedly envisaged the dispatch of 300,000 Chinese for permanent local residence. The implications of this project, according to the Soviets, were unmistakable: "Remembering Mao Tse-tung's long-standing aim to annex Mongolia to China and understanding perfectly what role these immigrants could play, the government of the MPR consented to admit a relatively small number of Chinese workers and for just a short period (between 1956 and 1964, 20,000 PRC citizens came to work in the MPR for various durations)."[48]

Mongolia was not the only pawn in this game, however. India also received much attention in light of its chronic border difficulties with the PRC. Vietnam has since entered the picture with the business of the Paracel and Spratly Islands. Soviet spokesmen have criticized the PRC's behavior toward North Korea as well, charging that "during the war in Korea certain leaders of the PRC did not want to take account of the Korean comrades who were courageously resisting aggression and behaved themselves rudely and arrogantly."[49] Going even farther, Soviet authors have made a point of the fact that:

> On March 8, 1963, *Jen-min jih-pao* came out with an article in which an attempt was made to justify China's territorial claims against neighboring countries. Together with other unequal treaties, the article likewise cited the 1895 treaty of Shimonoseki by which the Manchu Empire recognized the independence of Korea and lost Taiwan. In 1945 the question of China's ownership of Taiwan was finally resolved. The question that comes to mind is what is the meaning of the reference in 1963 to the provisions of the Shimonoseki treaty? Apparently, Peking has not lost hope to return the Koreans to the bosom of the "Chinese state."[50]

No matter what one thinks about the substantive merits of this welter of recriminations, the procedural consequences of the experiment leave no doubt. The decision to increase the cast and broaden the audience had the net effect of hardening the position of the Soviet Union and the PRC in their mutual affairs because of keen awareness that other states were watching the performance and/or waiting to see if they could turn to their own advantage any concession that the PRC wrung from the Soviet Union or vice versa. Fear of precipitating an avalanche of creditors has gradually rendered both Moscow and Peking reluctant to compose their differences on terms which the interested onlookers might impute to "softness," although, as previously noted, at the incipient stage of its career the PRC did toy with the notion that generosity vis-a-vis lesser adjacent countries on this score would be suitably rewarded.

By the same token, whenever Moscow championed the cause of a smaller neighbor against Peking and Peking reciprocated in kind, attitudes here were also profoundly affected for the reason that these subsidiary problems got entangled in the Sino-Soviet dispute and shared the fate of the primary contest. It is difficult to imagine that the Soviets and the Chinese ignored the definite probability that when either of them backed a third party against the other, the move served to drive a wedge between the principals, except, of course, where a prospect existed that by making a timely compromise the "client" might be wooed away from his initial sponsor. Again, the Chinese had tested that technique in the fifties, with a measure of success, but even they seem to have switched to a tougher line in recent years in pursuing their territorial ambitions, whereas the Soviets never evinced any inclination to relax their grip on what they thought themselves entitled to or to desist from pressing their claims to the uttermost limits. Indeed, it is worth emphasizing that the PRC's benevolence in this regard dates from an earlier era, so that the latest step of advertising the territorial problem between the Soviet Union and the PRC and seeking sympathy and support abroad appears to have made Peking more intransigent in its drive to recoup lost fragments of the ancestral estate and less eager to cultivate its original image of benign Big Brother.

TERRITORIAL DISPUTE VS. TERRITORIAL CONFLICT

Next, as a result of the Mao interview, a trend was inaugurated whereby the territorial conflict aspect of the controversy concerned with title to concrete pieces of land steadily assumed increasing prominence in the corresponding chapter and verse of the Sino-Soviet polemics at the expense of the territorial dispute item dealing with the pedigree of the current boundary line. Interestingly enough, although the Chinese are to blame for this phenomenon, it must be said in their defense that they bear only partial culpability for the subsequent course of events in this sector. In effect, a careful reading of the remarks attributed to Mao clearly shows a desire to dramatize the frontier issues between the Soviet Union and other states, while keeping the Sino-Soviet affair in the background. On the latter score, Mao reputedly was content to observe that "about a hundred years ago, the area to the east of [Lake] Baikal became Russian territory, and since then Vladivostok, Khabarovsk, and other areas have been Soviet territory," merely adding that "we have not yet presented our account for this list."[51] Compared with his emphatic endorsement of the right of other neighbors of the Soviet Union to the reversion of territory previously lost to the USSR, the statement on the Sino-Soviet question sounded completely noncommittal and must be seen as a conscious bid to maintain a low-key profile here in favor of letting other countries bask in the spotlight.

Once again, the Soviets refused to go along with the artifice and openly tried to pin the responsibility for this development on the Chinese by accusing Peking of advancing a claim to one and a half million square kilometers of Soviet territory.[52] The charge was both inaccurate and unfair, since apparently Mao went out of his way to avoid perpetrating that faux pas. Even so, the Soviets chose to interpret his words quite differently and, in the process, shifted the focus of the argument from the grand theme of the origins and legitimacy of the frontier to the plain business of ownership of particular parcels of land. However, Moscow too moved with caution and attempted to apply cosmetics to its actions. For, the official Soviet response to Mao's indictment, in the form of the aforementioned Pravda editorial, confined itself to a review of the historical record and a challenge to the evidentiary validity of historical memorabilia in support of demands for redrawing existing state frontiers. Technical rebuttal of the PRC's case was left to secondary sources,[53] a modus operandi which allowed the Soviets to articulate the merits of their own position in very explicit and adversary terms and yet to pretend that these were expressions of private opinion which did not bind the authorities and foreclosed no options for negotiation on alternate grounds.

Despite these safeguards, the accent on the territorial element of the equation to the detriment of its territorial dispute component had a significant impact on the tone of the communications exchanged between the rival capitals in that it logically ensued in the growing "juridification" of the relevant diplomatic syntax. Historical and ideological disquisitions on the genesis and evolution of frontiers usually rely on a rather amorphous legal scenario; by contrast, contentions over material goods favor resort to substantive legal rules.

In the first situation, the wavelengths are tuned to the language of politics; in the second instance, priority passes to legal style. The change in the nature of the contest, from macro- to micro-scale, is one explanation for the commensurate expansion of the role of legal artifacts in this context. Another reason lies in the gradual erosion of certain doctrinal inhibitions against such a procedure. Indeed, to the extent that in the past relations between the Soviet Union and the PRC were governed by the principles of socialist internationalism, international law was largely excluded from the picture. When they subsequently switched to the code of peaceful coexistence, the old constraints no longer applied, which meant that the ordinary norms of international law could presently be invoked in their mutual transactions, including those which pertained to territorial matters. Lifting the moral bar, then, in a sense served to legitimize the adoption in public of a litigational posture congruent with overt recourse to legal tools to promote each party's objectives.

A factor worth underlining at this point is that, as the above remarks indicate, the tissue of the Sino-Soviet territorial debate consists of two separate, albeit related, threads, respectively designated for the occasion as a territorial dispute and a territorial conflict. To be sure, the twin strands frequently intersect and throughout exert a profound influence upon one another, but, in terms of their roots, rationale, modus operandi, performance, and likely outcome, they remain clearly distinguishable and analytically severable. The territorial dispute is by far the more intriguing, raising, as it does, fundamental questions of doctrinal orthodoxy, diplomatic ethics, historical outlook, and political psychology. By contrast, the territorial dispute portion of the agenda features rather petty and routine arguments over proprietary rights. The format and substance of the dialogue reflect the disparate nature of the problems involved in each instance. The prize over which the territorial dispute is being waged is extremely tempting: the very magnitude of the stake, however, serves to defuse the situation and keeps the confrontation here essentially non-explosive because the level of risk that active pursuit of these goals would entail is, under normal circumstances, virtually unacceptable and the power to make such a decision vests in the highest rungs of the official hierarchy so as to minimize the possibility of stumbling into a full-fledged military crisis through local error or miscalculation. In short, the rewards are sorely tempting; yet neither side can really afford to gamble on the kind of operation that would be required properly to secure these ends. The desire may be present, but putting it into practice at this time appears to lie beyond both parties' inclination and/or capability. Of course, one should never entirely discount the element of human fallibility in the sense that a chance always exists that a blunder, or misapprehen-

THE 1964 CONFERENCE

sion of the opponent's true intentions, or a bout of irrationality will intrude to upset the most careful game plans; unpredictable developments apart, though, the prospect that the issues aired in the territorial dispute will precipitate a physical clash is quite remote, at least at the current stage.

The territorial conflict item is a completely different matter in this respect, for the topic is in fact intrinsically volatile and eminently lends itself to prompt and satisfactory solution by resort to force. The saving grace is that the bone of contention in this case seems so trivial by most reasonable standards that a major effort to assert ownership over these "assets" is hardly warranted. The impulse, in other words, may be strong in this context to settle the controversy by a show of might, but the potential gains are small enough to counsel prudence and moderation in conducting the experiment. The wide variance in the detonating quotient of the two components helps explain the marked change of attitude that stamped the discussions on the corresponding themes. Since the territorial dispute has a low flash-point, the record indicates that the contestants felt free to indulge in utterly vitriolic and unbridled public rhetoric on various aspects of the phenomenon in the presumed belief that their verbal excesses could produce no incendiary effect. As against this, the territorial conflict was handled gingerly precisely due to awareness of its flammable quality: the appropriate exchanges proceeded in secrecy, the claims were intangible, the charges were evasive, elaborate precautions were taken to treat the whole business as a common and minor affair that could best be attended to in an atmosphere of private negotiation devoid of any inkling of emotion or urgency, and consistently tight control was maintained over what was said and how it was phrased.

This is not to suggest that the subject of territorial dispute has only academic significance. Tactically speaking, the commodity has, it must be admitted, little visible relevance. The strategic implications are something else again. Merely because the PRC, for example, has not had the opportunity to take steps to implement its territorial thesis, that is, the grand territorial design, does not mean that the experience deserves to be dismissed as just an exercise in idle propaganda. Indeed, the indispensable legal groundwork was thereby laid for the positive assertion of the claims enunciated through this method if and when the propitious moment should occur. Given the ambitious nature of the goals, the occasion may never arise, for no less than a total collapse of Soviet power alone would enable the Chinese safely to test their "blueprint" for the virtual dismemberment of Russia's Asiatic domain. However, if the Paracel Islands episode constitutes a valid precedent, Peking may be quite prepared to wait patiently for the right chance here too, having amply established an image of what it may ultimately have in mind as a fair geographical modus vivendi on its northern flank versus the Soviet Union and, one should add, vis-a-vis Mongolia as well.

Nevertheless, the bid has incurred some danger in that the Chinese by their behavior may have unsheathed a double-edged sword and in the future might be called upon to pay dearly for their boldness. For, Moscow has countered Peking's script with its own dramatic version according to which it was the Manchu Empire that had committed a flagrant act of aggression against peaceful Russian settlements in the Amur valley, ending in the imposition of the terms of the unequal Treaty of Nerchinsk that ratified the unlawful Manchu occupation of the region south of the Amur River. Presumably, then, should the Chinese persist in unraveling the history of the boundary line in this area, the Russians had the prior option of impugning the legitimacy of the Nerchinsk <u>diktat</u> and demanding the "return" of a vast expanse of land across the Amur of which Russia had purportedly been illegally deprived by a treaty which could be pronounced null and void by the same criteria that the Chinese were invoking to question Soviet ownership of the territories on the opposite bank of that fluvial artery.

Whether or not the Chinese figured on this contingency is hard to tell. Even if they did, they still may have felt sufficiently cynical about the mores of the Soviet comrades to conclude that an extra alibi would make no difference in this case and that the Soviets could be expected to initiate that kind of a move, the situation permitting, without need of a convenient excuse by the Chinese to justify their insatiable appetite for territorial aggrandizement. At any rate, the type of notice the Chinese put the Soviets on concerning what lot might befall their Far Eastern possessions should the Soviet system falter has elicited an equivalent response whereby the Chinese have been informed that an analogous fate, mutatis mutandis, may be in store for their northern provinces should the PRC's statehood ever come to grief.

CONCLUSION

In closing, one supplementary observation may be in order. Assuming (which we do) that locutional usage offers a viable clue to underlying motives, a careful analysis of the public record from this alternate perspective only tends further to dispel the notion that the territorial element contributed a significant dimension to the Sino-Soviet controversy, at least at the incubating stage. Rather, the foregoing debate over frontiers bears every earmark of an intricate game played for extrinsic political stakes pursuant to a series of well-defined rules. Style is crucial: the parties show keen awareness of what can properly be said, how it should be worded, and that they must preserve throughout the exchange the principle of proportionality, lest the fixed limits of the colloquy be transcended and the contest unwittingly take on a riskier character than intended by the opponents. The territorial issue has undoubtedly helped inflame the tempers on both sides, nasty enough already, and so has aggravated the circumjacent politico-ideological struggle waged by Moscow and Peking, without, however, achieving a raison d'être of its own or gaining a stature sufficiently dominant to steer the overarching conflict into new and uncharted channels.

The role assigned to international law in the process fits the picture just outlined. The weapon of law was used sparingly during this initial phase, and for good cause. Law is rigid, and everybody concerned sought to maintain maximum flexibility of maneuver. Law deals with right and wrong and ascribes guilt and innocense. Amicable compromise held out a better promise of attaining success. Law means a collision at a state level, and the present <u>malentendu</u> was, by unanimous vote, still pictured as a quarrel between rival teams of dedicated Marxists-Leninists. Law has other defects as well. Arguments drawn from the fund of general international law are ideologically impure and, in any case, probably are out of place in a conversation between "fellow-socialists." And "socialist international law" sheds no light on the matter, for the very phenomenon which required a solution was a priori barred as an impossibility under the terms of membership in the "socialist commonwealth"—hence, the dilemma and the wispy quality of the legal accompaniment to the political recitatives. Note that even on those rare occasions where, as we have recently learned, genuine international legal formulas were invoked—the <u>thalweg</u> rule, for instance, during the 1964 negotiations—the fact was not made public until many years later. Granted, the rationale for citing the principle—the dispute over the status of the river islands—was itself at the time a relatively well-kept secret, but then one wonders if fear of precipitating a legal quarrel or of being caught breaking a doctrinal taboo or pilloried for introducing alien standards into a family "debate" was not perhaps a prime motive for maintaining the silence to begin with, since the topic could hardly be discussed intelligently without venturing into the legal sphere.

Yet, we can admire the performance as an impressive piece of orchestration or as a superlative essay in choreography. The trick is not to confuse drama with real life and, a fortiori, a plot's ornamental decor with its essence, thus rashly billing a sparring match as a deadly duel.

A striking aspect of the territorial dispute theme has been its durability. Of course, the territorial conflict issue gradually amplified the controversy, but the debate over the question of the validity of the old boundary line continues unabated, and the tone and tenor of the dialogue has remained remarkably consistent throughout. Indeed, the presistence of the affair is such that some explanation of this unusual phenomenon is called for.

Regardless of who started tossing the notion of a Sino-Soviet territorial dispute around, it soon became the property of the Chinese, and the Chinese are definitely responsible for having kept the topic alive all this time. The reasons for the problem's longevity must then be sought in the political and diplomatic agenda of the PRC leadership, and here several hypotheses recommend themselves.

First, to the extent that Peking had in the 1960s developed an intense interest in emancipating itself from Moscow's dominance as senior member of their partnership and has since retained that attitude, a territorial "feud" provided both the kind of solid crowbar that initially enabled the Chinese to pry themselves loose from the Soviet embrace and thereafter could serve as a cudgel to preserve a safe distance between the two erstwhile companions. In psychological and symbolic terms, perhaps no other artifact could so well convey the spirit of utter estrangement between the Soviet Union and the PRC than a public confrontation over the legitimacy of their common frontier. Since the Chinese were the ones who stood to gain from the "divorce," their stake in advertising the tangible evidence of alienation as proof of their complete independence made good sense. Nor has the scenario changed in that respect.

Second, Communist China has experienced a period of considerable inner turmoil, and the image of an external enemy often has, under the circumstances, acted as a convenient rallying cry. Promoting the Soviet threat to China's nationhood by, inter alia, painting the Russians as traditional despoilers of China's historical dominion was bound to appeal to Chinese patriotism and help reknit a country badly split by years of political turbulence. Furthermore, awareness of a vague and general peril might be even more effective as a means of engineering national unity than knowledge of a specific source of danger and certainly the menace of the Soviet Union was portrayed in sufficiently abstract fashion to generate the desired emotional revulsion without, however, giving rise to militant sentiments or panicky behavior that could cause practical difficulties for the PRC authorities in dealing with the Soviet Union or maintaining internal control. Add to this the persistence of factional strife within the PRC ruling circles and the distinct possibility that some local quarters still harbor sympathy for the Soviet Union or might contemplate aligning themselves with the Soviet Union in order to prevail in the struggle against their domestic opponents. In that context, vigorous denunciation of the Soviet Union for encroaching on PRC lands would go far toward discrediting on home ground any group likely to orient itself on Moscow either out of sincere conviction or opportunistic calculation.

Third, as the prospects for rapprochement with the United States improved, the need for the PRC to demonstrate its independent (adversary?) posture vis-a-vis the Soviet Union increased. From the PRC's point of view, conclusive evidence of friction between Peking and Moscow would plainly not be amiss in courting Washington's good will and probably no better way existed of convincing Washington that the PRC was worth cultivating than to show how sorely Peking's relations with Moscow were strained. It may, in fact, be suggested that the Chinese were in this case deliberately exploiting the peculiarities of the Western outlook which has a habit of treating territorial incidents as crises situations. To a U.S. statesman, for instance, a border dispute promptly conjures up the specter of war or at least a malignant condition of perpetual tension on the border which must wreck all hope of normal intercourse between the parties concerned until the intractable issue is, by some stroke of luck, resolved in a comparatively acceptable manner. There is reason to believe that the Chinese do not suffer from a similar territorial fixation and do not share this doomsday mentality on the subject of the absolute integrity of their territorial domain. Within the Chinese frame of reference, land can be traded for higher advantages, whereas it is virtually inconceivable for a European politician to operate on these premises. Thus, by engaging in a territorial argument with the Soviet Union, the Chinese were sure to impress the Americans as free spirits on the global scene and, by the same token, hasten the process of Sino-American detente.

Fourth, conscious of Soviet embroilment in unfinished border business with a number of neighboring countries, the Chinese saw a chance to generate sympathy for their own position by joining other states aggrieved by Soviet territorial aggrandizement at their expense. A bond of solidarity could be forged between these nations and the PRC by exploiting the theme that all of them had been dispossessed by the Soviet Union. The PRC's advertising of its territorial losses to the Soviet Union would let it enter the club of countries that might be willing to voice demands for adjustments in their existing boundary lines with the Soviet Union in their favor and enable the PRC, by posing as a fellow-victim, to stiffen the membership's resolve to press forward with such "revisionist" claims.

One trouble with this approach, of course, was that the PRC had not yet settled its own border problems with several adjacent countries and the resulting ambiguity could prove potentially embarrassing. Flaying the Soviet Union for its predatory practices without having first clarified how the Chinese intended to take care of pending border questions between themselves and various contiguous countries required considerable skill. What worked to Peking's benefit was the fact that the Soviet Union's intransigence on that score was already a matter of record, while the PRC had always sounded more flexible in that connection and soon took suitable steps to reenforce the reasonable image it here wished to project by making visible concessions in border negotiations staged with several nearby states. The combination of Soviet rigidity and PRC ambivalence on territorial items thus allowed Peking to harp on that theme with a measure of success, despite the handicap created by the sense of anxiety encountered among many of the PRC's neighbors stemming from uncertainty over how they will fare when the time comes to sit down with the PRC and discuss the topic of their common frontiers.

Inasmuch as these considerations are likely to last as a feature of long-term PRC foreign policy planning—barring unexpected changes of a rather dramatic nature—the border dispute with the Soviet Union seems destined to remain a valuable political asset in Peking's hands which it will be loath to forego, at least in the foreseeable future. The prospect then is for the diplomatic dialogue to continue at essentially the old pace, for the PRC has no real incentive to terminate the polemics and, indeed, appears to think that it stands to gain by prolonging the contest. Since the Soviet Union has no viable option to end the affair unilaterally, the show will run on. In similar vein, though, resort to mass force is also precluded, even assuming it ever represented a feasible alternative. At this juncture, the rationale of the territorial dispute lies in its very existence and the Chinese, as the principal architects of the controversy, must figure that precipitate action can offer no significant benefit and instead will probably hurt their efforts to use the territorial debate to maximum international advantage. True, the Soviets might be tempted to use physical power, but the Chinese have been careful not to provide them with a satisfactory excuse to do so on an adequate scale. Meanwhile, except that the battle of words quite obviously manages to grate on the Soviets' nerves, the latter do retain effective control of the territory which is the object of the argument and, unless strongly motivated to strike out, would attain little and risk a lot by letting rhetoric escalate into blows. In short, the odds favor the status quo to survive unimpaired.

NOTES

1. Edgar Snow's Interview with Chou En-lai, in Conakry, Guinea, January 23, 1964, New York Times, Feb. 3, 1964, pp. 1, 3.
According to M. I. Sladkovskii, Istoriya torgovo-ekonomicheskikh otnoshenii SSSR s Kitaem (1917-1974), Moscow, 1977, p. 298, the talks took place behind closed doors at the suggestion of the Chinese side.

THE 1964 CONFERENCE 133

   2. Dispatch from Tanjug International Service, Belgrade, February 27, 1964, in D. J. Doolin, Territorial Claims in the Sino-Soviet Conflict, Stanford, Hoover Institution Studies No. 7, 1965, p. 37. The Soviet and Chinese negotiating teams were headed, respectively, by a Soviet plenipotentiary with the rank of Deputy Minister, P. I. Zyryanov, and a Chinese Deputy Foreign Minister, Tseng Yung-tsun. See, Text of Statement by Soviet Government of March 29, 1969, Pravda, March 30, 1969, and Soviet News, 1969, No. 5483, pp. 3-4, 14.
   3. O. B. Borisov, B. T. Koloskov, op. cit., p. 304.
   4. How aware everybody was of this risk can be gathered from the noncommittal tone of Chou En-lai's statement to Edgar Snow, from which the world initially learned of the impending conclave: asked if the PRC had "any serious border disputes" with the Soviet Union or whether one could "regard existing boundaries as satisfactory to both parties and not subject to future negotiations," his cryptic reply was that "we have reached an agreement with the Soviet Union that negotiations be held on the Sino-Soviet boundary questions."
   5. New York Times, Feb. 26, 1964, p. 8. See, too, Colina MacDougall, "Rumanian Failure," Far Eastern Economic Review, 1964, No. 13, pp. 657-58.
   6. Report delivered by Mikhail Suslov to a plenary meeting of the Central Committee on February 14, 1964, World Communist Unity (Soviet Booklet No. 3), London, 1964, p. 31; Plenum Tsentral-nogo Komiteta Kommunisticheskoi Partii Sovetskogo Soyuza, 10-15 fevralya 1964 goda, stenograficheskii otchet, Moscow, 1964, p. 492.
   7. World Communist Unity, p. 59; Plenum, pp. 516-17. Cf., B. M. Klimenko, Gosudarstvennye granitsy-problema mira, Moscow, 1964, pp. 101-2.
   8. Asian Recorder, 1964, p. 5748.
   9. Soviet News, 1967, No. 5402, p. 107; Pravda, Sept. 1, 1967; Izvestiya, Sept. 2, 1967.
   10. Information Department of the Chinese Foreign Ministry, "Chenpao Island Has Always Been Chinese Territory," Peking Review, 1969, No. 11, p. 15 (hereafter abbr. as PR).
   11. PR, 1969, No. 17, p. 3. Cf., Statement of the Government of the People's Republic of China, May 24, 1969, PR, 1969, No. 22, p. 5.
   12. Statement of the Government of the People's Republic of China, May 24, 1969, PR, 1969, No. 22, p. 2.
   13. Regardless of what the Soviet negotiator at the conference may or may not have said concerning the location of the boundary line along the border rivers, Soviet sources maintain that the frontier follows the Chinese bank. See, for instance, A. Kruchinin, V. Olgin, Territorial Claims of Mao Tse-tung: History and Modern Times, Moscow, n.d., p. 72:

In 1861 (on June 16), upon the demarcation of the frontier in the territory, the parties signed an additional article of the Peking Treaty. In accordance with this article an exchange of maps, as mentioned in article 1 of the Peking Treaty, and bearing the state seals and signatures of the representatives of both parties, then took place.

In the region of Damansky Island the frontier runs directly along the Chinese bank of the Ussuri: An exchange of detailed maps with a description of the boundary line from the Ussuri to the sea also took place at that time. Authentic copies of the said documents are in possession of both the Soviet and the Chinese states.

Apparently, Soviet practice in the past has also observed this principle, for pro-Chinese sources have charged that "the Russians . . . have unilaterally decided that, when the unequal treaty they forced upon China says that the Heilunkiang (Amur) River should be the boundary, it means that the Russians possess the river right up to the Chinese bank!" See, G. Ginsburgs, "The Dynamics of the Sino-Soviet Territorial Dispute: The Case of the River Islands," in J. A. Cohen (ed.), The Dynamics of China's Foreign Relations (Cambridge, Mass: Harvard East Asian Monographs No. 39, 1970), p. 3.

14. Pravda, Mar. 30, 1969; Izvestiya, Mar. 30, 1969; USSR Government Statement of March 29, 1969, Moscow, 1969, p. 13.

15. Statement of the USSR Government of June 13, 1969, Pravda, June 14, 1969; Izvestiya, June 14, 1969; Soviet News, 1969, No. 5494, p. 139.

16. A. Kruchinin, V. Olgin, op. cit., pp. 94-95.

As against this, consider the evidence of Soviet statements that by the time Mao made his famous statement to the visiting Japanese delegation on July 10, 1964, the Soviet and Chinese negotiators were engaged in trying to introduce clarity into the maps and had almost finished determining what questions would be discussed. After Mao's "intervention," which the Soviets describe as having been clearly intended to put difficulties in the way of the negotiations, the Chinese reportedly refused to exchange maps on which had already been marked the sections of the frontier on which agreement had previously been reached. M. I. Sladkovskii, op. cit., p. 298.

17. I. Aleksandrov, "Peking and Soviet-Chinese Relations," Pravda, Apr. 28, 1976, reproduced in Socialism: Theory and Practice,

THE 1964 CONFERENCE 135

June, 1976, Suppl., p. 32; New York Times, Dec. 24, 1974, p. 5, and Apr. 29, 1976, p. 10; "Statement of the Government of the People's Republic of China, May 24, 1969," China Reconstructs, 1969, No. 7, Suppl., p. 3 (hereafter abbr. as CR); Down with the New Tsars! Soviet Revisionists' Anti-Chinese Atrocities on the Heilung and Wusuli Rivers, Peking, 1969, n.p.; V. S. Olgin, "Ekspansionizm v pogranichnoi politike Pekina," Problemy Dalnego Vostoka, 1975, No. 1, p. 39.

18. Adam W. Wysocki, "Soviet-Chinese Border Talks, Separating the Facts from the Fantasy," Zycie Warszawy, reproduced in Soviet News, 1974, No. 5744, p. 254.

> Only four years later did the Soviets put out this version under their own name. See, "Realnost i vymysly, K voprosu o sovetsko-kitaiskom pogranichnom uregulirovanii," Pravda, Apr. 1, 1978, pp. 4-5: "In 1964, at the Soviet initiative, Soviet-Chinese consultations were held to clarify the location of the line of the frontier in particular sectors. During the consultations, the delegations exchanged topographic maps. And then there was discovered that on the Chinese maps a whole row of segments of Soviet territory was assigned to China and the line of the frontier in these sectors was arbitrarily drawn deep in Soviet territory, behind that line which Soviet border guards had watched from the time of the creation of the Soviet state. It is precisely these portions of Soviet territory that the Chinese side designated as 'disputed'."

19. USSR Government Statement of March 29, 1969, p. 8. Incidentally, Damansky Island was specifically identified as the scene of armed conflict with the Japanese overlords of Manchuria. See, Geroi Ostrova Damanskii, Moscow, 1969, p. 18.

20. USSR Government Statement of March 29, 1969, p. 9. Also, A. Kruchinin, V. Olgin, op. cit., pp. 91-92. Indeed, according to O. B. Borisov, B. T. Koloskov, Sovetsko-Kitaiskie otnosheniya 1945-1970, kratkii ocherk, Moscow, 1971, even as late as 1966, the Soviet authorities responded favorably to Chinese requests to permit citizens of the PRC access to islands belonging to the Soviet Union and to the Soviet waters of the border rivers for economic activities, to allow Chinese peasants to drive their herds through the territory of the Soviet Union, and so on.

21. "Statement of the Government of the People's Republic of China, May 24, 1969," CR, 1969, No. 7, Suppl., p. 1. In similar vein, "Statement by the Foreign Ministry of the PRC of Mar. 11, 1969," New York Times, Mar. 12, 1969, p. 16; Down with the New Tsars!,

n. p.; PR, 1969, No. 17, p. 3; Strong Protest Against the Soviet Revisionists' Intrusion into China's Territory (CR, 1969, No. 3), pp. 3, 5: Chenpao (Damansky) Island "has always been under China's jurisdiction and patrolled by Chinese frontier guards since long ago."

22. Text in Sbornik deistvuyushchikh dogovorov, soglashenii i konventsii, zaklyuchennykh SSSR s inostrannymi gosudarstvami, Moscow, 1957, Vol. 14, pp. 333-36.

23. Statement of the Government of the USSR of June 13, 1969, Pravda, June 14, 1969.

24. "Statement of the Government of the People's Republic of China, May 24, 1969," CR, 1969, No. 7, Suppl., p. 4.

25. S. G. Yurkov, G. P. Petrov (eds.), Vneshnepoliticheskie kontseptsii Maoizma (pravovye aspekty), Moscow, 1975, p. 216.

26. A. W. Wysocki, loc. cit. The author adds:

> The Chinese side wrecked the consultations in 1964 by refusing, despite the mutual arrangement, to go to Moscow to continue them, and the agreement reached was never made an official document.
>
> The Soviet side has repeatedly proposed over the past three years that agreement be reached on the eastern part of the border and that the frontier line on the border sections of the rivers be drawn along the channel. Moreover, the Soviet side has proposed that a draft agreement on the eastern border sector be worked out with regard for the consultations of 1964, which, taking the interests of both sides into account, would fix the line of the new border along the fairway on the navigable rivers and along the middle of the non-navigable rivers. The Soviet Union has submitted a thoroughly worked out draft of such an agreement, and it lies on the table of the Chinese.
>
> Peking has refused even to discuss the Soviet proposal, rejecting it outright.

27. Pravda, June 14, 1969; Soviet News, 1969, No. 5494, p. 139.

28. Statement of the Government of the People's Republic of China (October 7, 1969), Peking, 1969, pp. 44-45.

29. Sbornik deistvuyushchikh dogovorov, soglashenii i konventsii, zaklyuchennykh SSSR s inostrannymi gosudarstvami, Moscow, 1956, Vol. 13, pp. 262-65.

30. See, M. M. Avakov, Pravopreemstvo Sovetskogo gosudarstva Moscow, 1961, p. 101.

31. Sovetsko-Afganskie otnosheniya 1919-1969gg., dokumenty i materialy, Moscow, 1971, p. 102.

32. It is, of course, curious that the PRC government never invoked the USSR-Afghanistan precedent on its own behalf in the polemics with the Soviet Union regarding the line of the frontier in the Amur and Ussuri Rivers. One possible explanation may be that the Chinese just did not know about the episode. Another reason could be that the Chinese did not wish to put themselves in a position of being beholden to Russian bounty, as the Afghanis obviously had no objections doing, and to obtain what they considered their clear right as an act of Soviet dispensation. The latter attitude would fit the general pattern of Chinese behavior in this connection and thus the interpretation has much to recommend it.

33. PR, 1964, No. 19, p. 13.
34. Ibid.
35. Asian Recorder, 1964, p. 5748.
36. PR, 1964, No. 19, p. 13.
37. Ibid.
38. See D. J. Doolin, op. cit., pp. 38-39.
39. Ibid., pp. 39-40. Also, Asian Recorder, 1964, p. 5807. The same theme recurs in Izvestiya, May 31, 1964; condensed text in English in Current Digest of the Soviet Press, 1964, No. 23, pp. 3-4: "Observance of sovereignty and equal rights in deeds and not in words means: respect for the laws, practices and traditions that have become established in this or that socialist country; respect for the government and party authorities to whom the people have entrusted the administration of the country; and respect for historically evolved state borders. The Chinese authorities are crudely trampling on all these elementary norms of relations between sovereign states."

40. D. J. Doolin, op. cit., pp. 40-41.
41. O. B. Borisov, B. T. Koloskov, op. cit., pp. 302-3.
42. Vneshnyaya politika i mezhdunarodnye otnosheniya Kitaiskoi Narodnoi Respubliki 1963-1973, Moscow, 1974, Vol. 2, p. 33.
43. Sekai Shūhō, Tokyo, Aug. 11, 1964, excerpted in D. J. Doolin, op. cit., pp. 42-44. Also, Pravda, Sept. 2, 1964.
44. "In connection with Mao Tse-tung's talk with a group of Japanese Socialists," Pravda, Sept. 2, 1964.
45. A. S. Tsvetko, Sovetsko-Kitaiskie kulturnye svyazi, istoricheskii ocherk, Moscow, 1974, pp. 101-2 (emphasis in original).
46. Harry Schwartz, "Rumania Borrows a Leaf from de Gaulle," New York Times, May 16, 1966, p. 36.
47. Yomiuri Shimbun, Tokyo, July 13, 1964, cited in D. J. Doolin, op. cit., pp. 44-45.
48. Vneshnyaya politika KNR, O sushcnosti vneshnepoliticheskogo kursa sovremennogo kitaiskogo rukovodstva, Moscow, 1971, p. 58.
49. S. G. Yurkov, Pekin: Novaya politika? Moscow, 1972, pp. 25-26.

50. S. G. Yurkov, G. P. Petrov (eds.), op. cit., p. 201. Also, Vneshnyaya politika KNR, p. 58.

The events of the Cultural Revolution have furnished the Russians with fresh ammunition in this connection. According to Vneshnyaya politika i mezhdunarodnye otnosheniya Kitaiskoi Narodnoi Respubliki 1963-1973, Vol. 2, p. 146, for instance, "in December 1968 and March 1969 there were incidents on the Chinese-Korean frontier." Similarly, S. G. Yurkov, G. P. Petrov (eds.), op. cit., p. 37, describe how during the Cultural Revolution, the Chinese staged forays across the frontier against populated areas in the DPRK, installed loud speakers along their entire border to broadcast threats and insults to the DPRK and its leaders and succeeded in terrorizing the local population.

51. As cited in D. J. Doolin, op. cit., p. 44.

52. In Connection with Mao Tse-tung's Talk with a Group of Japanese Socialists, Moscow, n.d., p. 10.

53. Notably, V. M. Khvostov, "Kitaiskii 'schet po reestru' i pravda istorii," Mezhdunarodnaya zhizn', 1964, No. 10, pp. 21-27.

The fact that this important essay was not featured in the English-language edition of the journal (International Affairs) has prompted considerable speculation as to the meaning of the omission. In our opinion, this step fits the pattern of Soviet efforts to downplay the "legal" replies to Mao's "provocation" and confine this part of the debate to "domestic channels." To be sure, the Russian version was also accessible to the outside world and thus did act to advertise the Soviet thesis, but managed to achieve the desired end discreetly.

SELECTIVE BIBLIOGRAPHY

BOOKS AND PAMPHLETS

An, Tai Sung, The Sino-Soviet Territorial Dispute. Philadelphia: Westminster Press, 1973.

Avakov, A. A. Pravopreemstvo Sovetskogo gosudarstva. Moscow, 1961.

Barsegov, Yu. G. Territoriya v mezhdunarodnom prave. Moscow, 1958.

Bettati, Mario. Le Conflit Sino-Soviétique. Vol. 2: Le Conflit entre Etats. Paris: Armand Colin, 1971.

Blaustein, A. P., ed. Fundamental Legal Documents of Communist China. South Hackensack, N. J.: Rothman and Co., 1962.

Blishchenko, I. P. Antisovetizm i mezhdunarodnoe pravo. Moscow, 1968.

Borisov, O. B. and Koloskov, B. T. Sovetsko-Kitaiskie otnosheniya 1945-1970, kratkii ocherk. Moscow, 1971.

A Call for a Treaty Renouncing the Use of Force in the Settlement of Territorial and Frontier Disputes. Soviet Booklet, Vol. 2, No. 2. London, 1964.

Chasovye dalnikh rubezhei. Moscow, 1970.

Chicherin, G. V. Stat'i i rechi po voprosam mezhdunarodnoi politiki. Moscow, 1961.

Cohen, J. A. and Chiu, H., eds. People's China and International Law, A Documentary Study. 2 volumes, Princeton, N. J.; Princeton University Press, 1974.

A Comment on the Statement of the Communist Party of the U. S. A. Peking, 1963.

Dallin, A., ed. Diversity in International Communism, A Documentary Record, 1961-1963. New York: Columbia University Press, 1963.

Deklaratsii, zayavleniya i kommyunike Sovetskogo pravitelstva s pravitelstvami inostrannykh gosudarstv 1954-1957gg. Moscow, 1957.

Doolin, D. J. Territorial Claims in the Sino-Soviet Conflict. Hoover Institution Studies No. 7. Stanford, 1965.

Down with the New Tsars! Soviet Revisionists' Anti-China Atrocities on the Heilung and Wusuli Rivers. Peking, 1969.

Gavrilov, I. Duplicity (on double-dealing policy of Peking splitters). Moscow, n.d.

Geroi Ostrova Damanskii. Moscow, 1969.

Ginsburgs, G. The Damansky/Chenpao Island Incidents: A Case Study of Syntactic Patterns in Crisis Diplomacy. Asian Studies: Occasional Paper Series, no. 6 (Gene T. Hsiao, ed.). Southern Illinois University at Edwardsville, 1973.

Griffith, W. E. Sino-Soviet Relations, 1964-1965. Cambridge, Mass., and London: MIT Press, 1966.

Hsiung, J. C. Law and Policy in China's Foreign Relations, A Study of Attitudes and Practice. New York and London: Columbia University Press, 1972.

Important Documents of the First Plenary Session of the Chinese PPCC. Peking, 1949.

In Connection with Mao Tse-tung's Talk with a Group of Japanese Socialists. Moscow, 1964.

Kabanov, P. I. Amurskii vopros. Blagoveshchensk, 1959.

Kapitsa, M. S. Eskalatsiya verolomstva (Politika Pekina i Sovetsko-Kitaiskie otnosheniya). Moscow, 1970.

_____. KNR: dva desyatiletiya-dve politiki. Moscow, 1969.

_____. Levee zdravogo smysla (O vneshnei politike gruppy Mao). Moscow, 1968.

SELECTIVE BIBLIOGRAPHY

_____. Sovetsko-Kitaiskie otnosheniya. Moscow, 1958.

Keesing's Research Report. The Sino-Soviet Dispute. New York: Charles Scribner's sons, 1969.

Khrushchev, N. S. The Present International Situation and the Foreign Policy of the Soviet Union. Soviet Booklet No. 104, December. London, 1962.

Kitai segodnya. Moscow, 1969.

Klimenko, B. M. Gosudarstvennye granitsy-problema mira. Moscow, 1964.

_____ and Ushakov, N. A. Nerushimost granits—uslovie mezhdunarodnogo mira. Moscow, 1975.

Kovalev, E. F., ed. Zakonodatelnye akty Kitaiskoi Narodnoi Respubliki. Moscow, 1952.

Kruchinin, A. and Olgin, V. Territorial Claims of Mao Tse-tung: History and Modern Times. Moscow, n.d.

Leninskaya politika SSSR v otnoshenii Kitaya. Moscow, 1968.

Mennens, C. The Soviet Point of View in the Sino-Soviet Conflict. Ghent: Slavica Gandensia 2, 1975.

Molodtsov, S. Peace to Frontiers! Moscow, 1965.

Obrazovanie Kitaiskoi Narodnoi Respubliki, dokumenty i materialy. Moscow, 1950.

The Origin and Development of the Differences between the Leadership of the CPSU and Ourselves. Peking, 1963.

Plenum Tsentralnogo Komiteta Kommunisticheskoi Partii Sovetskogo Soyuza, 10-15 fevralya 1964 goda. stenograficheskii otchet. Moscow, 1964.

Pod znamenem proletarskogo internatsionalizma, sbornik materialov. Moscow, 1957.

Pommerening, H. Der Chinesisch-Sowjetische Grenzkonflikt, Das Erbe der ungleichen Verträge. Walter-Verlag: Olten und Freiburg, 1968.

Prokhorov, A. K voprosu o Sovetsko-Kitaiskoi granitse. Moscow, 1975.

A Reply to Peking. Soviet Booklet No. 122. London, 1963.

Russko-Kitaiskie otnosheniya v XVII veke, materialy i dokumenty. 2 volumes. Moscow, 1969-1972.

Savvin, V. P. Vzaimootnosheniya tsarskoi Rossii i SSSR s Kitaem, 1619-1927. Moscow, 1930.

Shapiro, L., ed. Soviet Treaty Series. 2 volumes. Washington, D. C.: Georgetown University Press, 1950-1955.

Shevtsov, V. S. National Sovereignty and the Soviet State. Moscow, 1974.

Smolenskii, P. Diplomatiya i granitsy. Moscow, 1965.

Snow, E. Red Star over China. rev. ed. New York: Random House, 1938.

Sovetsko-Afganskie otnosheniya 1919-1969gg., dokumenty i materialy. Moscow, 1971.

Sovetsko-Kitaiskie otnosheniya, 1917-1957, sbornik dokumentov. Moscow, 1959.

Statement of the Government of the People's Republic of China (October 7, 1969). Peking, 1969.

Tang, Peter S. H. Russian Expansion into the Maritime Province: The Contemporary Soviet and Chinese Communist Views. Washington, D. C.; Research Institute on the Sino-Soviet Bloc, 1962.

Tsvetko, A. S. Sovetsko-Kitaiskie kulturnye svyazi, istoricheskii ocherk. Moscow, 1974.

USSR Government Statement of March 29, 1969. Moscow, 1969.

Vice-Premier Chen Yi Answers Questions Put by Correspondents. Peking, 1966.

Vneshnyaya politika i mezhdunarodnye otnosheniya Kitaiskoi Narodnoi Respubliki 1949-1973. 2 volumes. Moscow, 1974.

Vneshnyaya politika KNR, O sushchnosti vneshenpoliticheskogo kursa sovremennogo kitaiskogo rukovodstva. Moscow, 1971.

Watson, F. The Frontiers of China. New York: Praeger, 1966.

Whiting, A. S. Soviet Policies in China, 1917-1924. New York: Columbia University Press, 1954.

World Communist Unity. Soviet Booklet No. 3. London, 1964.

Yurkov, S. G. Pekin: novaya politika? Moscow, 1972.

_____. and Petrov, G. P., eds. Vneshnepoliticheskie kontseptsii Maoizma (pravovye aspekty). Moscow, 1975.

Zadorozhnyi, G. P. Granitsam—mir! Moscow, 1964.

Zanegin, B. Nationalist Background of China's Foreign Policy. Moscow, n.d.

Zasedaniya Verkhovnogo Soveta SSSR shestogo sozyva, vtoraya sessiya (10-13 dekabrya 1962g.). stenograficheskii otchet, Moscow, 1963.

Zinner, P. E., ed. National Communism and Popular Revolt in Eastern Europe. New York: Columbia University Press, 1956.

ARTICLES

Andersen, V. "Neravnopravnye dogovora Tsarskoi Rossii s Kitaem v XIX veke." Borba klassov 1936, No. 9: 102-12.

Beskrovnyi, L. G. and Narochnitskii, A. L. "K istorii vneshnei politiki Rossii na Dalnem Vostoke v XIX veke." Voprosy istorii 1974, No. 6: 14-36.

_____. Tikhvinskii, S., and Khvostov, V. "K istorii formirovaniya Russko-Kitaiskoi granitsy." Mezhdunarodnaya zhizn' 1972, No. 6: 14-29.

Blishchenko, I. "Mezhdunarodnoe pravo i mirnoe razreshenie sporov." Novoe vremya 1964, No. 7: 9-11.

Chiu, H. "Certain Legal Aspects of Communist China's Treaty Practice." American Society of International Law Proceedings 1967, pp. 117-26.

Denisov, A. "Geograficheskie 'izyskaniya' Pekina." Novoe vremya 1972, No. 33: 15.

Dmitriev, B. "Granitsy gosudarstv i uprochenie mira." Mirovaya ekonomika i mezhdunarodnye otnosheniya 1964, No. 3: 17-26.

Durdenevskii, V. N. "Sovetskaya territoriya v aktakh mezhdurnarodnogo prava za 30 let (1917-1947gg.)." Sovetskoe gosudarstvo i pravo 1947, No. 12: 58-65.

Frenzke, D. "Der Begriff des ungleichen Vertrages im sowjetisch-chinesischen Grenzkonflikt." Osteuropa-Recht 1965, No. 2: 69-105.

Ginsburgs, G. "The Dynamics of the Sino-Soviet Territorial Dispute: The Case of the River Islands." In J.A. Cohen, ed., The Dynamics of China's Foreign Relations, Harvard Asian Monographs No. 39, pp. 1-20. Cambridge, Mass., 1970.

Grigor'eva, E. A., Kostikov, E. D. "Spekulyatsiya maoistov ponyatiem 'neravnopravnyi dogovor'." Problemy Dalnego Vostoka 1975, No. 1: 48-58.

Ivanov, K. "National Liberation and Territorial Conflicts." International Affairs 1964. No. 5: 8-14.

Ivanov, O. "Soviet-Chinese Relations: Truth and Fiction." Socialism: Theory and Practice 1975, No. 1 (Suppl.): 45-61.

Khvostov, V. M. "Kitaiskii 'schet po reestru' i pravda istorii." Mezhdunarodnaya zhizn' 1964, No. 10: 21-27.

Kostikov, E. D. "Politicheskaya kartografiya na sluzhbe velikoderzhavnogo natsionalizma." Problemy Dalnego Vostoka 1973, No. 4: 85-93.

_____. "Velikoderzhavnye ambitsii i pogranichnaya politika pekinskogo rukovodstva." Problemy Dalnego Vostoka 1973, No. 1; 53-62.

Kozhevnikov, F. and Piradov, A. "Mezhdunarodnoe pravo i vopros o granitsakh." Kommunist 1964, No. 2: 32-38.

Krivtsov, V. A. "Maoizm i velikokhanskii shovinizm kitaiskoi burzhuazii." Problemy Dalnego Vostoka 1974, No. 1: 74-87.

Kryazhev, A. Ya. "Izvrashchenie maoistami leninskoi natsionalnoi politiki." Izvestiya Sibirskogo otdeleniya Akademii Nauk SSSR. seriya obshchestvennykh nauk 1976, No. 1 (vyp. 1): 99-105.

Molodtsov, S. "Frontiers and International Law." International Affairs 1964, No. 4: 9-14.

_____. "Mirnoe uregulirovanie territorialnykh sporov i voprosov o granitsakh." Sovetskii ezhegodnik mezhdunarodnogo prava. 1963, pp. 70-84.

Monconduit, F. "La Note Khrouchtchev du 31 décembre 1963 relative au règlement pacifique des litiges territoriaux." Annuaire français de droit international, 1964, pp. 38-63.

Myasnikov, V. S. "Russian-Chinese Relations in the Seventeenth Century (documents and materials)." Mimeographed.

Nikolayev, F. "How Peking Falsifies History." International Affairs 1973, No. 5: 28-34.

Olgin, V. S. "Ekspansionizm v pogranichnoi politike Pekina." Problemy Dalnego Vostoka 1975, No. 1: 36-47.

Yurkov, S. G. "50 let Sovetsko-Kitaiskikh otnoshenii." Problemy Dalnego Vostoka 1974, No. 2: 63-75.

Zorin, V. A. and Israelyan, V. L. "Marksistsko-leninskii podkhod k Resheniyu Territorialnykh sporov." Kommunist 1964, No. 2: 23-31.

ABOUT THE AUTHORS

GEORGE GINSBURGS is Professor of Foreign and Comparative Law, Rutgers University. He has published numerous books and articles on international law and diplomatic affairs, often focusing on Soviet legal and political issues. His most recent work is a volume coedited with Alvin Z. Rubinstein, <u>Soviet Foreign Policy Toward Western Europe</u> (Praeger, 1978).

CARL F. PINKELE is Assistant Professor of Politics and Government at Ohio Wesleyan University. He has coauthored an earlier monograph with Dr. Ginsburgs on Sino-Soviet relations and has also written articles on political issues in the United States.

RELATED TITLES
Published by Praeger Special Studies

SOVIET-ASIAN RELATIONS IN THE 1970s AND BEYOND:
An Interperceptional Study
         Bhabani Sen Gupta

DIMENSIONS OF CHINA'S FOREIGN RELATIONS
         edited by Chün-tu Hsüeh

SOVIET NATIONALITY POLICIES AND PRACTICES
         edited by Jeremy R. Azrael

THE SOVIET THREAT: MYTHS AND REALITIES
         edited by Grayson Kirk
         and Nils Wessell

INDIVIDUAL RIGHTS AND THE STATE IN FOREIGN
AFFAIRS: An International Compendium
         edited by Elihu Lauterpacht
         and John G. Collier

SOVIET FOREIGN POLICY TOWARD WESTERN
EUROPE
         edited by George Ginsburgs
         and Alvin Z. Rubinstein